REVISE 11+

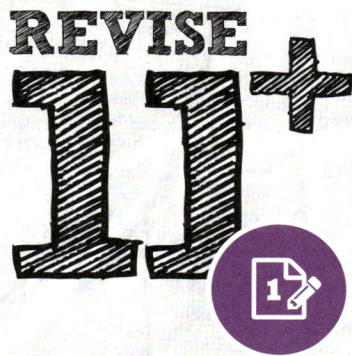

Also available to support
Maths 11+ revision:

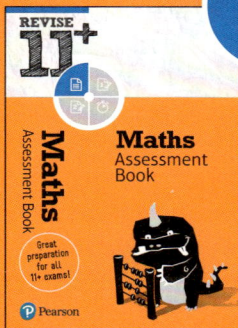

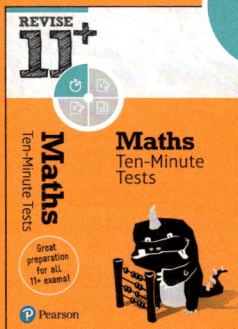

REVISE 11+
Maths Practice Book 2
Maths
Practice
Book 2
Great preparation for all 11+ exams!
Pearson

REVISE 11+
Maths Assessment Book
Maths
Assessment
Book
Great preparation for all 11+ exams!
Pearson

REVISE 11+
Maths Ten-Minute Tests
Maths
Ten-Minute
Tests
Great preparation for all 11+ exams!
Pearson

Maths
Practice
Book 1

Series Consultant: Harry Smith
Author: Rebecca Corden

THE REVISE 11⁺ SERIES

For the full range of Pearson Revise 11+ titles visit:
www.pearsonschools.co.uk/revise11plus

Pearson

Contents

How to use this book   1

Diagnostic test   2

Number

1 Ordering and rounding numbers   8

2 Negative numbers   12

3 Decimal numbers   16

Calculation

4 Mental addition and subtraction   20

5 Column addition and subtraction   24

6 Multiplication   28

7 Division   32

Checkpoint 1   36

Fractions, decimals and percentages

8 Fractions   38

9 Percentages   42

10 Equivalence   46

Ratio and proportion

11 Ratio and proportion   50

12 Scale factors   54

Checkpoint 2   58

Shape and measurement

13 Converting units   60

14 Perimeter   64

15 Area   68

16 Reflections and translations   72

Checkpoint 3   76

Progress test   78

Answers   84

Progress chart   102

How to use this book

Complete the *Diagnostic test*.

Diagnostic test

Complete this test before you start any of the practice sections. It covers all the topics in this book and is as hard as a real 11+ test, so don't worry if you get a lot of answers wrong. It will help you see which topics you need to practise the most.

1 Write these numbers in order, starting with the lowest.
  63 023   64 978   897 001   6309
  → Section 1

2 Round
  a 5678 to the nearest 10
  b 67 100 to the nearest 1000
  c 721 458 to the nearest 100
  → Section 1

3 Circle the number that is the difference between −5 and 10
  −15   5   15   −5
  → Section 2

4 Look at these numbers.
  −10   −8   5   2   −7   8   −6
  Write down the:
  a lowest value _____
  b highest value _____
  c second lowest value _____
  → Section 2

Read the *Before you begin* box and study the *Worked examples*.

In the 11+ test you might be asked to put large numbers significant figure.

Before you begin

Ordering numbers using place value

When you order numbers, you must consider:
- The number of digits
- The place value of those digits

	Millions	Hundreds of thousands	Tens of thousands	Thousand
a	7	6	6	3
b	7	6	9	1

Use the hints and support to answer the *Guided questions*.

Guided questions

1 Joe has bought a jumper costing £29.99 and some trouse How much has he spent in total?

  £ 2 9 . 9 9
+ £ 1 3 . 9 9
  £ ☐ ☐ . 9 8

£ _____

2 Work out 26 828 + 13 457

  2 6 8 2 8
+ 1 3 4 5 7
  ☐ ☐ ☐ 8 5

3 Work out 25 846 − 12 475

  2 5 8 4 6
− 1 2 4 7 5

Complete the *Timed practice* in test conditions.

Timed practice

1 Calculate 5678 ÷ 6
  Give your answer as a whole number and a r
  _____

2 Divide these numbers.
  a 456 ÷ 10 = _____
  b 63.25 ÷ 100 = _____
  c 98 564 ÷ 1000 = _____
  d 500.1 ÷ 100 = _____

3 George pays £96 for 24 pots of paint. Each

Work independently in the *Have a go* section. The orange difficulty dials will tell you how challenging each question is.

Have a go

1 Find the missing numbers.
  a 512 + _____ = 624
  b 498 − _____ = 250
  c 631 + 635 = _____
  [3 marks]

2 Complete these calculations.
  a 7281 + 4000 = _____
  b 29 845 + 6000 = _____
  c 85 963 − 500 = _____
  d 270 496 − 92 = _____
  [4 marks]

Take a break with *Beyond the exam* activities.

53 456	53 460	a

Beyond the exam

When you are shopping in the s money you have spent. This is v would be rounded to £2

Track your progress on the *Progress chart* and follow the instructions in the *Time to reflect* box.

c The third most popular ba

Time to reflect

Mark your *Timed practice*

Check your answers in the back of th

☐ **0—11 marks**
  Scan the QR code for extra
  Then, move on to the next practic
  try Test 1 in the Ten-Minute Tests

Practise mixed questions in the *Checkpoints*.

Checkpoint 1

In this checkpoint, you will practise skills from the **Number** and **Calculation** topics. There are 16 questions for you to answer.

1 Circle the number with the lowest value.
  89 001   89 010   89 100   89 110
  → Section 1

2 Write the numbers in order, starting with the lowest.
  43 036   4536   430 036   43 630
  → Section 1

3 Complete the table by rounding these numbers as shown.
  → Section 1

Number	Nearest 10	Nearest 100	Nearest 1000
75 562	75 560	b _____	76 000
12 002	12 000	12 000	c _____
9987	a _____	10 000	10 000

4 On Monday, the temperature is −2°C. On Tuesday, it is 3 degrees warmer than it was on Monday. Circle Tuesday's temperature.
  −5°C   −1°C   1°C   0°C
  → Section 2

5 Identify the missing temperatures.
  → Section 2

6 Complete the sequence.
  0.05   0.07   0.09   _____   0.13   _____
  → Section 3

Complete your revision with the *Progress test*.

Progress test

Complete this test once you have worked through all the practice sections in this book. It covers all the topics in this book and is as hard as a real 11+ test.

1 Write these numbers in order from highest to lowest.
  89 897   89 798   894 798   8948
  → Section 1

2 Round
  a 8238 to the nearest 1000
  b 587 115 to the nearest 100
  c 9998 to the nearest 100
  → Section 1

3 In Moscow, the temperature is −12°C. In Rome, the temperature is 30°C. How much warmer is it in Rome than Moscow?
  _____ °C
  → Section 2

4 Write these numbers in order from lowest to highest.
  −15   12   −8   −5
  → Section 2

5 Circle the false statement.
  a 5.63 to the nearest whole number = 6   b 3.019 to the nearest hundredth = 3.02
  c 0.214 to the nearest tenth = 0.2   d 5.689 to the nearest tenth = 5.6

Move on to Practice Book 2

Diagnostic test

Complete this test before you start any of the practice sections. It covers all the topics in this book and is as hard as a real 11+ test, so don't worry if you get a lot of answers wrong. It will help you see which topics you need to practise the most.

45

1 Write these numbers in order, starting with the lowest.

| 1 | mark |

Section 1

    63 023   64 978   697 001   6309

_____   _____   _____   _____

2 Round

| 3 | marks |

Section 1

a 5678 to the nearest 10   _____

b 67 100 to the nearest 1000   _____

c 723 458 to the nearest 100   _____

3 Circle the number that is the difference between −5 and 10

| 1 | mark |

Section 2

−15   5   15   −5

4 Look at these numbers.

Section 2

−10   −8   5   2   −7   8   6   −6

Write down the:

a lowest value   _____

b highest value   _____

| 3 | marks |

c second lowest value   _____

5 Circle the pair of numbers which complete the sequence: 0.20, 0.22, 0.24, _____ , _____

| 1 | mark |

Section 3

0.26 and 0.27   0.26 and 0.28   0.27 and 0.28   2.6 and 2.8

6 Round

Section 3

a 9.63 to the nearest whole number   _____

b 3.012 to the nearest hundredth   _____

| 3 | marks |

c 9.264 to the nearest tenth   _____

7 Use the bus timetable to complete the statements.

Bus number	Departure time	Arrival time
210	11:03	13:01
7	12:41	15:30
230	09:32	10:30
63	10:17	10:52

Section 3

a The bus number with the longest journey is: _____

b The bus number with the second longest journey is: _____

2 marks

8 Write these Roman numerals in modern numbers.

Section 4

a XCIII = _____

b MD = _____

2 marks

9 A car salesperson sells one car for £5358 and another for £8632 What is the total amount of money she receives?

Section 5

£ _____

1 mark

10 There are 5086 spaces in a car park and 1874 are filled. How many spaces are empty?

Section 5

_____

1 mark

11 Complete the chart.

Section 6

Number	÷ 10	÷ 100	÷ 1000
562	56.2	**a** _____	0.562
4897	**b** _____	48.97	**c** _____

3 marks

12 Entry to the funfair is £2.99 per person. How much does Sarah pay for a group of 4 people?

Section 6

£ _____

1 mark

13 Calculate 50×40

Section 7

_____

1 mark

14 Calculate $562 \div 14$

Section 7

Give your answer as a whole number and a remainder.

_____

1 mark

15 There are 324 boxes in a warehouse. 12 boxes fit on a truck. How many truck loads will it take to transport all the boxes?

Section 7

1 mark _____

16 Write $1\frac{1}{5}$ as an improper fraction.

Section 8

1 mark _____

17 Simplify each fraction.

a $\frac{2}{16}$ = _____

b $\frac{4}{40}$ = _____

3 marks

c $\frac{5}{25}$ = _____

18 Complete the table.

Section 9

Percentage	Decimal	Fraction
2%	**a** _____	$\frac{2}{100}$
b _____	0.99	$\frac{99}{100}$
11%	0.11	**c** _____

3 marks

19 Clare has 500 chickens and 80% of them lay eggs. How many chickens do not lay eggs?

Section 9

1 mark _____

20 Mrs Smith has a garden full of tulips. 10% of them are purple, $\frac{3}{10}$ are red. The rest are orange. What percentage of tulips are orange?

Section 10

1 mark _____ %

21 Circle the values below that are equivalent to $\frac{2}{10}$

Section 10

1 mark

    2%   20% $\frac{4}{5}$ 0.2

22 In a park, there are two types of tree: oak and pine. 25 are pine and 75 are oak.
What is the ratio of pine trees to oak trees? Give your answer in its simplest form.

Section 11

1 mark

_____

23 Divide 150 into the following ratios.

Section 11

2 marks

    a 1 : 2 _____ and _____   **b** 3 : 2 _____ and _____

24 What scale factor has been used to enlarge this shape?

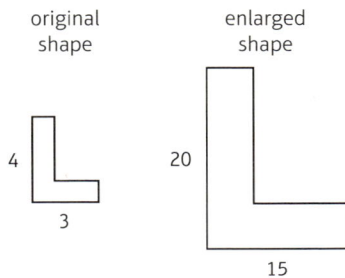

Section 12

original
shape

enlarged
shape

4

20

3

15

1 mark

_____

25 A race track has a length of 200 m and a width of 30 m. It is enlarged using a scale factor of 1.5
What are the new measurements of the race track?

Section 12

length = _____ m

width = _____ m

2 marks

26 Convert 1900 ml to litres.

Section 13

_____ litres

1 mark

27 Harry's foot is 11 inches long. Approximately how many centimetres is this?
Circle the correct length.

Section 13

1 mark

    11 cm   22 cm   27.5 cm   30 cm

28 Suri cycles 3 miles to school. Approximately how many kilometres is this? Circle the best answer.

Section 13

1 mark

    4 km   6 km   4.5 km   30 km

29 Henry's homework takes him quarter of an hour each night for three nights.
Circle the total amount of time Henry has spent on his homework.

Section 13

1 mark

    45 minutes   1.15 hours   0.45 hours   0.25 hours

30 A square diving pool has sides of 12 m. What is its perimeter?

Section 14

1 mark

_____ m

31 Find the perimeter of this shape in metres.

Section 14

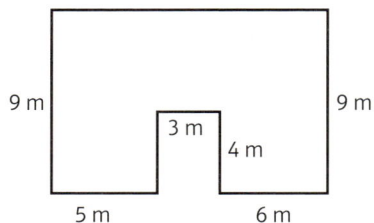

1 mark

_____ m

32 A playground is 39 m long by 18 m wide. What is its area?

Section 15

1 mark

_____ m²

33 List these shapes in order from the smallest area to the largest area.

Section 15

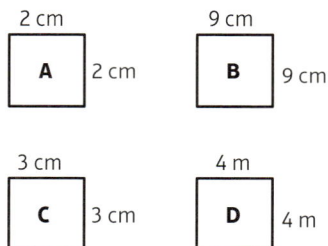

1 mark

_____   _____   _____   _____

34 Describe the translation of this shape.

Section 16

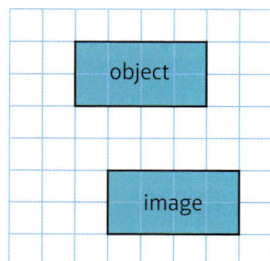

1 mark

_____

35 Plot the following coordinates and draw the shape: (3, −2) (3, 2) (4, 3) (4, −3)

Section 16

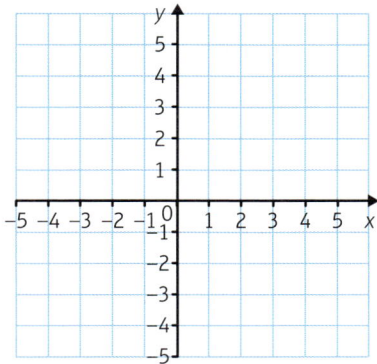

1

mark

36 Complete the statement.

Section 16

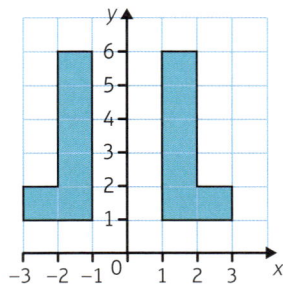

The shape has been reflected in the ＿＿＿＿＿＿ axis.

1

mark

Time to reflect

Mark your *Diagnostic test* out of 52. How did you do?

☐ *0–44 marks*
Start your 11+ preparation by beginning at practice section 1 and working through the whole book.

☐ *45–52 marks*
Use the section links to identify your strengths and weaknesses. You could start by looking at the practice sections you scored the lowest in.

1 Ordering and rounding numbers

In the 11+ test you might be asked to put large numbers in order. You may also need to round whole numbers to a given significant figure.

Before you begin

Ordering numbers using place value

When you order numbers, you must consider:

- The number of digits
- The place value of those digits.

123 A whole number with more digits is worth more than one with fewer digits. Digits have a **greater value** as you work towards the **left**.

	Millions	Hundreds of thousands	Tens of thousands	Thousands	Hundreds	Tens	Ones
a	7	6	6	3	2	1	5
b	7	6	9	1	2	1	5

The number in **example a** has 5 ones and only 1 ten, but the ten still has a higher value.

This digit tells us how many millions each number has. It has the **largest value**.

The number in **example a** has 6 tens of thousands, so it is **worth less** than the number in **example b** which has 9 tens of thousands. Both numbers have the same amount of millions and hundreds of thousands.

You can write the number in **example a** in **words** like this: seven million, six hundred and sixty three thousand, two hundred and fifteen. You can write it in **figures** like this: 7 663 215

Rounding numbers

You can use **place value** to decide whether to round **up** or **down**.

To round to the nearest 10, look at the **ones** column.

To round to the nearest 100, look at the **tens** column.

To round to the nearest 1000, look at the **hundreds** column.

To round to the nearest 10 000 look at the **thousands** column.

To round to the nearest 100 000 look at the **tens of thousands** column.

123 If the number in the column you are looking at is **5 or higher, round up**.

If the number in the column you are looking at is **lower than 5, round down**.

578**6** → 579**0**   Rounding to the nearest 10: the new number will have one zero in the units column.

57**8**6 → 58**00**   Rounding to the nearest 100: the new number will have a zero in the tens column and a zero in the units column.

5**7**86 → 6**000**   Rounding to the nearest 1000: the new number will have zeros in the hundreds, tens and units columns.

Worked examples

1 Use the symbols < or > to show which numbers in these pairs are greater or lesser.

9399 $>$ 9356   The first number has more tens.

89 658 $<$ 89 758   The first number has fewer hundreds.

2 Fill in the chart by rounding the number to the nearest 10, 100, 1000 or 10 000

Number	Nearest 10	Nearest 100	Nearest 1000	Nearest 10 000
56 854	56 850	56 900	57 000	60 000

123 > means 'is greater than' and < means 'is less than'.

Guided questions

1 Rob is rounding numbers. He says 'I will round 56 871 to 56 900'

Are these statements true or false? Tick the correct column.

	True	False
A Rob has rounded his number to the nearest ten.	☐	✓
B Rob has rounded his number to the nearest hundred.	☐	☐
C Rob has rounded his number to the nearest thousand.	☐	☐

> If rounded to the nearest ten, the number would have a 7 in the tens column.

> This number rounded to the nearest thousand becomes 57 000

2 What is the number 55 378 rounded to the nearest 1000? Circle the correct answer.

~~55 400~~   56 678   55 000   56 000

> This is 55 378 rounded to the nearest 100. We need to look at the **hundreds** column when rounding to the nearest 1000

> **123** Numbers rounded to the nearest 1000 will end in at least 3 zeros.

3 Circle the number with the lowest value.

46 654   45 465   ~~466 456~~   45 665

> This number has 6 digits, the others have 5 so they have a lesser value.

> When ordering larger whole numbers, look at the number of digits first. Then check the value of the digits, starting from the **left**.

4 Complete the table by rounding the number.

> Use your knowledge of rounding rules to find the nearest 100 and 1000

Number	Nearest 10	Nearest 100	Nearest 1000	Nearest 10 000
53 456	53 460	**a** _____	**b** _____	50 000

> Numbers rounded to the nearest 100 will end in at least 2 zeros.

Beyond the exam

When you are shopping in the supermarket, round prices to the nearest pound to keep an estimate of how much money you have spent. This is very useful for items that are priced just under the nearest pound. For example, £1.99 would be rounded to £2

Have a go

1 Write these numbers in order, starting with the highest.

| 32 000 | 56 899 | 5889 | 320 | 320 000 | 56 898 |

_____ _____ _____ _____ _____ _____

1 mark

> Look at the number of digits first. Next, check the **value** of each digit from **left to right.**

2 The table below shows the annual ticket sales of four different football clubs.

Club	Number of tickets sold
Kentville Utd	154 897
Bluefields Utd	163 496
Redrover FC	154 654
Northwood Rangers	101 899

a The club that sold the most tickets is: _____

b The club with the second highest ticket sales is: _____

2 marks

> Remember to check the value of digits starting from the **left.**

3 Round 43 897 to the nearest:

100	1000	10 000
a _____	b _____	c _____

3 marks

> Use rounding rules to decide whether to round up or down.

4 Sally rounds 638 768 to 639 000. Which of these best describes her rounding? Tick **one** option.

☐ Rounded to the nearest hundred

☐ Rounded to the nearest thousand

☐ Rounded to the nearest hundred thousand

☐ Rounded to the nearest ten

1 mark

> Look at the number of zeros and the digits that have changed.

Time to reflect

Mark your *Have a go* section out of 7. How are you doing so far?

Check your answers in the back of the book and see how you are doing.

☐ **Had a go**
0–3 marks

Have another look at the *Worked examples* on page 8. Then try these questions again.

☐ **Nearly there**
4–6 marks

Look at your incorrect answers. Make sure you understand how to get the correct answer.

☐ **Nailed it!**
7 marks

Congratulations! Now see whether you can get full marks on the *Timed practice*.

When you are ready, try the *Timed practice* on the next page.

Timed practice

⏱ **10**

1 Round

   a 8586 to the nearest 10 _____

   b 851 987 to the nearest 10 000 _____

   c 952 to the nearest 100 _____

   d 555 555 to the nearest 100 000 _____

4 marks

2 Identify how the following numbers have been rounded.

   a 3567 is 4000 to the nearest _____ .

   b 39 647 is 39 600 to the nearest _____ .

   c 371 596 is 370 000 to the nearest _____ .

   d 56 897 is 60 000 to the nearest _____ .

4 marks

3 Steve says, 'I have 96 pence. This rounds to 100, so I can afford something that costs £1'
Is he correct? Circle the correct answer.

yes   no

1 mark

4 Write these numbers in order, starting with the lowest.

   456 357   824 675   26 344   751 259   456 375   260 231

   _____ _____ _____ _____ _____ _____

1 mark

5 Look at the concert ticket sales for these bands.

Band	Ticket sales
Black Purple	45 897
Star Kittens	22 854
Cosmic Duo	39 897
Magic Dust	45 899

   a The band who sold the most tickets is _____ .

   b The band who sold the fewest tickets is _____ .

   c The third most popular band is _____ .

3 marks

Time to reflect

Mark your *Timed practice* section out of 13. How did you do?

Check your answers in the back of the book and write your score in the progress chart.

☐ **0–11 marks**
Scan the QR code for extra practice.
Then, move on to the next practice section or try Test 1 in the Ten-Minute Tests book.

☐ **12–13 marks**
Well done!
Move on to the next practice section or try Test 1 in the Ten-Minute Tests book.

2 Negative numbers

In the 11+ test, you will need to be able to order negative numbers. You also need to know how to add and subtract with them.

Before you begin

Negative numbers

Negative numbers are numbers that are **lower than zero**. They are sometimes called 'minus numbers'.

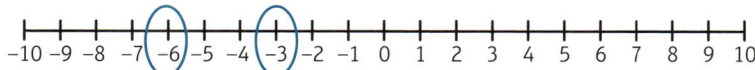

-10 -9 -8 -7 -6 -5 -4 -3 -2 -1 0 1 2 3 4 5 6 7 8 9 10

Number lines are useful when adding and subtracting negative numbers.

Negative numbers have a **minus** sign in front of them.

Negative numbers with a higher digit are lower than negative numbers with a lower digit.
For example, -6 is **lower** than -3
You can write this as $-6 < -3$

Numbers above zero are called **positive** numbers.

Worked examples

1   Add the missing numbers on the number line.

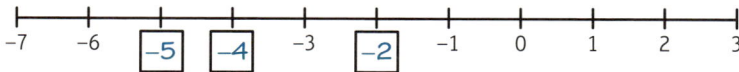

-7 -6 $\boxed{-5}$ $\boxed{-4}$ -3 $\boxed{-2}$ -1 0 1 2 3

2   Circle the lowest number in each bubble.

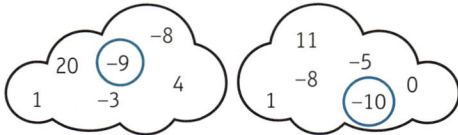

Bubble 1: 20, -8, $\boxed{-9}$, 4, 1, -3

Bubble 2: 11, -8, -5, 1, $\boxed{-10}$, 0

3   Between midnight and 3am, the temperature drops by $12\,°C$ from a starting point of $10\,°C$. Circle the temperature at 6am.

$-12\,°C$ $\boxed{-2\,°C}$ $22\,°C$ $-10\,°C$

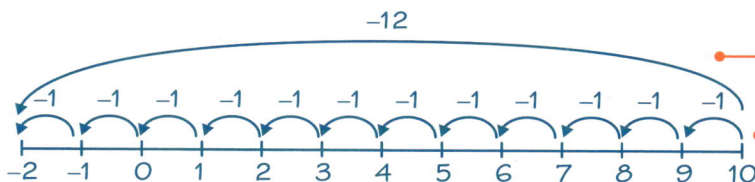

If the temperature drops, this means it gets lower.

Temperature can be measured in degrees celsius, which you write as '°C'.

-12

-1 -1 -1 -1 -1 -1 -1 -1 -1 -1 -1 -1

-2 -1 0 1 2 3 4 5 6 7 8 9 10

You could draw a number line to help you.

Count back 12 from 10 to reach -2

Beyond the exam

Use the internet to investigate temperatures in cold locations in the world. What is the coldest recorded temperature you can find?

Guided questions

1 Complete this sequence:

−10, __−8__, −6, _____, −2, 0, __2__, 4, 6, 8, _____

> This sequence is counting in steps of 2

2 Identify the temperatures shown by labels **A**, **B**, and **C** on the thermometer.

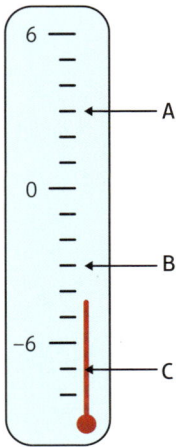

A _____ 3 _____ °C   **B** _____ °C

C _____ °C

> Each small division on the thermometer scale is worth 1 °C.

3 A bag of peas is kept at −2 °C in the freezer. When removed, they warm up by 5° in 5 minutes. What is the new temperature of the peas?

_____ °C

> Count up in ones from −2. When you add a positive number to a negative number, you move towards 0.

4 This chart shows the average summer and winter temperatures of some countries.

Country	Summer temperature in °C	Winter temperature in °C
Russia	16	−15
Canada	22	−5
Norway	18	−9

What is the difference in **degrees celsius** between the summer and winter temperatures in these countries.

a Russia _____ °C

b Canada _____ 27 _____ °C

> Count how many degrees above zero the summer temperature is, then how many degrees below zero the winter temperature is. Add these values together to find the difference.

5 Tick true or false for the following statements. Use the number line to help you.

	True	False
a −5 °C is one degree colder than −4 °C.	☐	☐
b 6 °C < five degrees warmer than −1 °C.	☐	☑
c 4 degrees below 2 °C is colder than −7 °C.	☐	☐

> If you add 5 to −1, you reach 4
> 4 is not more than 6, so **b** is false.

> = means equal to, < means less than, > means greater than.

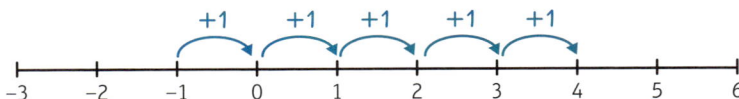

Have a go

1 Circle the highest number in each group.

a −5   9   −8   1

b 9   −9   −18   12

c −6   −3   −5   −8

> Remember negative numbers with a higher digit have lower values.

2 Complete these number sequences.

a −10, −8, _____, −4, −2

b −5, −10, −15, _____, −25

c 1, 0, _____, −2, _____, −4

> To find the missing numbers, work out what size steps the sequence uses.

3 George's garden thermometer reads −7 °C on Tuesday. On Wednesday, it is 5 degrees warmer. Complete the sentence below.

On Wednesday, the thermometer reads _____ °C.

> Draw a number line to help you visualise the calculation.

4 Circle the four lowest numbers.

−10   2   0   −3   4   −17   10   17

> The negative numbers must be lower than the positive numbers.

5 The table shows the lowest temperatures that three freezers can reach.

Model	Lowest temperature in °C
Super Freeze Model 9	−16
Ice Maker Deluxe	−4
Snow Time Freezer	−2

What is the difference in degrees between the coldest and warmest freezers?

_____ °C

Beyond the exam

Look at the food items in your freezer and find out what temperature each food should be stored at. List the items in order, starting with those that need to be coldest.

Time to reflect

Mark your *Have a go* section out of 9. How are you doing so far?

Check your answers in the back of the book and see how you are doing.

☐ **Had a go**
0–4 marks

Have another look at the *Worked examples* on page 12. Then try these questions again.

☐ **Nearly there**
5–8 marks

Look at your incorrect answers. Make sure you understand how to get the correct answer.

☐ **Nailed it!**
9 marks

Congratulations! Now see whether you can get full marks on the *Timed practice*.

When you are ready, try the *Timed practice* on the next page.

Timed practice

⏱ 10

1 Circle the warmest temperature and the coldest temperature.

−3 °C   −6 °C   5 °C   −7 °C   2 °C   −8 °C   4 °C

1 mark

2 Add the missing numbers to the number line.

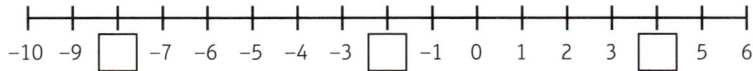

−10 −9 ☐ −7 −6 −5 −4 −3 ☐ −1 0 1 2 3 ☐ 5 6

1 mark

3 Use < and > to complete these statements.

a −1 ☐ 7

b −6 ☐ −10

c −8 ☐ −4

d −12 ☐ −21

4 marks

4 Circle the temperature that is 7 degrees warmer than −10 °C.

−2   −17   3   −3   7

1 mark

5 Use the number line to complete the following calculations.

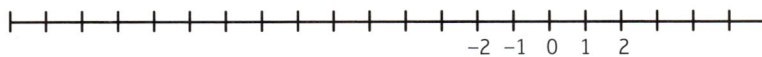

−2 −1 0 1 2

a Add 3 to −9   _____

b Add 6 to −2   _____

c Subtract 5 from 3   _____

d Subtract 3 from −8   _____

4 marks

6 The temperature of three different locations is measured at two different times during the day. Complete the chart, circling the correct answer to show the temperature change.

Location	Reading 1 in °C	Reading 2 in °C	Change in °C
1	−2	3	**a** _____
2	**b** _____	7	+6
3	−5	**c** _____	+10

3 marks

7 The seawater under the ice at the North Pole is −7 °C in December. If the water warms by 1 °C each month, what will the temperature be in March?

_____ °C

1 mark

Time to reflect

Mark your *Timed practice* section out of 15. How did you do?
Check your answers in the back of the book and write your score in the progress chart.

☐ *0–13 marks*
Scan the QR code for extra practice.
Then, move on to the next practice section or try Test 2 in the Ten-Minute Tests book.

☐ *14–15 marks*
Well done!
Move on to the next practice section or try Test 2 in the Ten-Minute Tests book.

3 Decimal numbers

In the 11+ test, you will need to be able to order and round decimal numbers.

Before you begin

Ordering decimal numbers

Decimal numbers represent tenths, hundredths, thousandths, and so on.

	Ones	Decimal point	Tenths $\frac{1}{10}$	Hundredths $\frac{1}{100}$	Thousandths $\frac{1}{1000}$
a	4	.	3	7	2
b	4	.	4	2	1

Just like whole numbers, decimal digits have less value as you work from left to right. Hundredths are worth less than tenths, and thousandths are worth less than hundredths. The number in row **b** has a greater value than the number in row **a** as it has 4 tenths.

You can use the digits after the **decimal point** to help you order decimal numbers.

Rounding decimal numbers

Round decimal numbers in the same way you round whole numbers.

4.67**2** → 4.6**7**

> To round to the nearest hundredth, look at the thousandths.

4.6**7**2 → 4.**7**

> To round to the nearest tenth, look at the hundredths.

4.**6**72 → **5**

> To round to the nearest whole number, look at the tenths.

123 The digits to the right of the decimal point show how many decimal places the number has. Both examples have **3 decimal places** (3 d.p.).

Look at practice section 1 to revise how to round numbers. If the number in the column you are looking at is lower than 5, round **down**.

123 The rule is: 5 or higher, round **up**, lower than 5, round **down**.

Worked examples

1 Circle the decimal with the **lowest** value.

1.546   1.654   1.564   (1.456)

> All these numbers have **one whole** so we must look at the **decimal digits** to compare them.

> This number has the **fewest** tenths so it is the number with the **lowest** value.

2 Who has written the larger number, Maria or Taz?

Maria	Taz
2.123	2.3

> Both numbers have the same digit in the ones column, but Taz's number has more tenths, so it is larger.

Taz

3 What is 3.546 rounded to the nearest hundredth? Circle the correct answer.

3.547   (3.55)   3.4   3.54

> There are 6 thousandths so the hundredths digit rounds **up** from 4 to 5

Guided questions

1 Circle the decimal with the highest value.

0.0012   0.010   0.01   0.1   0.011   0.0011

> Look at the **tenths** column to identify which number has the highest value.

2 Kamila has written a sequence. Which two decimal numbers are missing? Circle the correct option.

10.05   10.07   _____   10.11   10.13   _____   10.17

A 10.09 and 11.15
B 10.07 and 10.17
C 10.09 and 10.15
D 1.09 and 10.15

> To complete the sequence you need to count on in jumps of 2 hundredths.

> This pair of decimals already appears in the sequence.

3 Here are the times four athletes took to complete a 100 m race.

Name	Time in seconds
Nasreen	11.56
Tomas	11.02
Louise	11.20
Steve	11.59

a The fastest runner was _____ .

b The slowest runner was _____ .

c The runner in third place was _____ .

> The higher numbers represent slower times and the lower numbers represent quicker times.

4 Complete the table by rounding the decimals to the nearest whole number, tenth, hundredth and thousandth.

Number	Nearest whole number	Nearest tenth	Nearest hundredth
125.266	**a** _____125_____	125.3	**b** _____
63.261	63	**c** _____	**d** _____
5.625	6	**e** _____	5.63
2.996	**f** _____	3.0	**g** _____

> A number rounded to the nearest tenth will have no digits in the hundredths or thousandths place, meaning it will have 1 decimal place.

> When rounding up from 9, increase the digit to the left by 1

5 Mike's car can hold 65.29 litres of petrol in its fuel tank. What is this volume of petrol rounded to the nearest litre?

_____ litres

> Your answer will be a **whole number**.

Beyond the exam

Write down ten different decimal numbers that can be made from these number cards and a decimal point.

| 0 | 5 | 8 | 1 | • |

Now write your numbers in order, starting with the smallest.

Have a go

1 mark

1 Circle the decimal number with the lowest value.

2.598   2.958   2.9   2.095   2.895   20.298

2 Class 5 is practising for sports day. Their teacher has recorded the students' race times. Circle the names of the three fastest students.

Name	Time in seconds
Ben	35.13
Aziz	35.12
Tim	36.02
Alba	30.58
Malik	35.31
Will	35.21

> Check the place value of the digits starting from the left.

1 mark

3 Round

> Think carefully about the number of **decimal places** each answer will require.

a 1.23 to the nearest tenth   _____

b 3.258 to the nearest hundredth   _____

c 0.689 to the nearest whole number   _____

d 1.339 to the nearest tenth   _____

4 marks

4 Jack is buying new sports kit and rounds up the prices of the items he buys as he puts them in his basket. Complete the table.

Item	Actual price	Nearest pound	Nearest 10 pence
Football socks	£4.59	£5.00	**a** £_____
Drinks bottle	£2.42	**b** £_____	£2.40
Shin pads	£8.69	£9.00	**c** £_____

> Your answers should show pounds and pence with **2 decimal places.**

3 marks

1 mark

5 Circle the correct number sentence.

$3.20 < 3.02$ $5.5 = 2.5 + 2$ $6.3 > 0.6 \times 10$ $0.5 < 0.50$

6 Tick the **two** options that are equal to 65

    ☐   **A** 65.9 rounded to the nearest whole number

    ☐   **B** 64.99 rounded to the nearest tenth

    ☐   **C** 6.499 rounded to the nearest hundredth

    ☐   **D** 65.22 rounded to the nearest whole number

2 marks

Time to reflect

Mark your *Have a go* section out of 12. How are you doing so far?

Check your answers in the back of the book and see how you are doing.

☐ **Had a go**
0–5 marks
Have another look at the *Worked examples* on page 16. Then try these questions again.

☐ **Nearly there**
6–11 marks
Look at your incorrect answers. Make sure you understand how to get the correct answer.

☐ **Nailed it!**
12 marks
Congratulations! Now see whether you can get full marks on the *Timed practice.*

When you are ready, try the *Timed practice* on the next page.

Timed practice

10

1 Write these numbers in order, starting with the lowest.

    5.622   562.2   5.256   56.25

_____   _____   _____   _____

1 mark

2 Write these numbers in order, starting with the highest.

    0.222   2.002   0.002   0.020

_____   _____   _____   _____

1 mark

3 Round 4.562 to the nearest:

a tenth   _____

b hundredth   _____

c whole number   _____

3 marks

4 Complete these statements.

a 63.25 to 63.3 is rounded to the nearest _____ .

b 75.268 to 75.27 is rounded to the nearest _____ .

c 9.001 to 9 is rounded to the nearest _____ .

d 3.51 to 3.5 is rounded to the nearest _____ .

4 marks

5 Sally rounds a number to the nearest tenth and gets 3.6
Circle the **two** numbers she could have started with.

    3.57   3.33   3.03   3.61

2 marks

6 Alice and her brother and sister buy some presents for their dad. The presents cost £24.99, £26.99 and £14.99
They each guess how much the total is. Who is most accurate? Write **one** name on the answer line.

Alice says, 'We have spent roughly £67'

Jenny says, 'We have spent roughly £80'

Barney says, 'We have spent roughly £65'

_____

1 mark

Time to reflect

Mark your *Timed practice* section out of 12. How did you do?
Check your answers in the back of the book and write your score in the progress chart.

☐ *0—10 marks*
Scan the QR code for extra practice.
Then, move on to the next practice section or
try Test 3 in the Ten-Minute Tests book.

☐ *11—12 marks*
Well done!
Move on to the next practice section or try
Test 3 in the Ten-Minute Tests book.

4 Mental addition and subtraction

In the 11+ test, you will need to be able to add and subtract numbers up to 6 digits using mental methods. You can jot down workings to help you.

Before you begin

Mental addition and subtraction

Many calculations can be done using mental methods including:

1 Partitioning

261 + 357

200 + 300 = 500
60 + 50 = 110
1 + 7 = 8
618

Split the number up by place value first.

2 Near doubles or halves

24 + 25
24 ≈ 25

25 + 25 = 50
50 − 1 = 49

Use doubles and halves to add or subtract.

3 Chunking

966 − 9

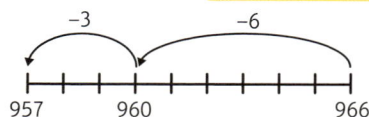

Count up or down in chunks up to the nearest 10, 100 or 1000 and then to the number you need.

−3   −6
957 960   966

4 Multiples of ten

235 − 78
78 ≈ 80

235 − 80 = 155
155 + 2 = 157

*Use **multiples of ten** and then adjust.*

123 The symbol ≈ is used to show approximate equivalence.

Roman numerals

When working out years in Roman numerals, you need to know what the letters stand for.

I	V	X	L	C	D	M
1	5	10	50	100	500	1000

VIII = 8, XXV = 25, LIV = 54, MMXVIII = 2018

1 Repeated letters are added together. For example, III = 1 + 1 + 1 = 3. V, L and D never repeat. Letters can only be repeated 3 times in succession.

2 If there is a larger-value letter before a smaller one, add them together. For example, XV = 10 + 5 = 15

3 If there is a smaller-value letter before a larger one, subtract the smaller from the larger one. For example, XC = 100 − 10 = 90

Worked examples

1 Henry VIII reigned from MDIX. Write this year in modern numbers.

1509

MD means 1000 + 500 = 1500
IX means 10 − 1 = 9

1 mark

2 Work out 483 − 321

483 − 300 = 183
183 − 20 = 163
163 − 1 = 162
162

Use chunking. Subtract 300, then 20, then 1 to reach the answer.

1 mark

Guided questions

1 Calculate $89\,564 + 68\,521$

$$80\,000 + 60\,000 = 140\,000$$
$$9000 + 8000 =$$
$$500 + 500 = 1000$$
$$60 + 20 =$$
$$4 + 1 =$$

_____

> Add the result of all the calculations together to get the final answer.

2 Sadie's old car is worth £950 but she accepts an offer of £60 less than this. How much does she sell her car for?

> Count down to the nearest 100 Subtract £50 from £950 to get £900, then subtract a further £10

£ _____

3 Farmer John has 448 chickens. Farmer Fatima has 450 chickens. How many chickens do they have together?

> Use a near double to find the answer: 448 is nearly 450, so double this number and subtract 2

_____

4 What is the missing number in this calculation?

> You can use the opposite operation when solving a missing number problem. Instead of adding, you need to subtract.

_____ $+ 202 = 652$

> You need to work out $652 - 202$

5 John sees these Roman numerals on the date stone of a house: MDCCCIX In what year was the house built?

> M = 1000
> DCCC = 500 + 100 + 100 + 100

_____

> Your date will need 4 digits, but one will be zero because there are no tens values.

6 Write these dates using Roman numerals to complete the chart.

Event	Modern numbers	Roman numerals
Battle of Hastings	1066	**a** MLXVI
Queen Elizabeth II born	1926	**b** MCMXXVI
Apollo 11 lands on the moon	1969	**c** _____

> M = 1000
> LXVI = 50 + 10 + 5 + 1 = 66

> M = 1000, CM = 1000 − 100 = 900
> XXVI = 10 + 10 + 5 + 1 = 26

123 The Romans did not generally use a numeral for zero.

Beyond the exam

Look for Roman numerals in real life and practise converting them into modern numbers. Examples can be found in film or TV credits, on clocks and on some old statues and buildings. Try converting the year of your birth into Roman numerals.

Have a go

1 Find the missing numbers.

a 512 + _____ = 624

b 498 − _____ = 250

c 631 + 635 = _____

3 marks

2 Complete these calculations.

a 7281 + 4000 = _____

b 29 845 + 6000 = _____

c 85 963 − 500 = _____

d 270 496 − 92 = _____

4 marks

3 Write these Roman numerals in modern numbers.

a VII = _____

b XCVI = _____

c CDIX = _____

3 marks

4 There are 2461 cans of beans and 1610 cans of peas in a supermarket. How many cans are there altogether? Circle the correct answer.

471   2622   4071   21 071

1 mark

5 Complete the calculation.

386 248 + 5006 = _____

1 mark

6 Find the missing number.

_____ + 4021 = 9759

1 mark

Time to reflect

Mark your *Have a go* section out of 13. How are you doing so far?

Check your answers in the back of the book and see how you are doing.

☐ **Had a go**
0–6 marks
Have another look at the *Worked examples* on page 20. Then try these questions again.

☐ **Nearly there**
7–12 marks
Look at your incorrect answers. Make sure you understand how to get the correct answer.

☐ **Nailed it!**
13 marks
Congratulations! Now see whether you can get full marks on the *Timed practice.*

When you are ready, try the *Timed practice* on the next page.

Timed practice

10

1 Complete these calculations.

a 830 + 560 = _____

b 456 + 147 = _____

c 854 − 133 = _____

d 897 − 345 = _____

4 marks

2 Complete these calculations.

a 2502 + 2503 = _____

b 999 + 999 = _____

c 249 − 125 = _____

d 998 − 500 = _____

4 marks

3 Complete the table.

Roman numerals	Modern numbers
CXCVII	**a** _____
b _____	569
c _____	1011

3 marks

4 A car park can hold 9547 cars when full. If 8596 cars are already parked, how many spaces are still available?

_____

1 mark

5 Complete these calculations.

a 340 − 92 = _____

b 854 − 72 = _____

c 613 + 127 = _____

3 marks

6 Find the missing numbers in these calculations.

a _____ + 960 = 1460

b 890 − _____ = 352

c 4897 + _____ = 5012

3 marks

Time to reflect

Mark your *Timed practice* section out of 18. How did you do?

Check your answers in the back of the book and write your score in the progress chart.

☐ *0–16 marks*
Scan the QR code for extra practice.
Then, move on to the next practice section or try Test 4 in the Ten-Minute Tests book.

☐ *17–18 marks*
Well done!
Move on to the next practice section or try Test 4 in the Ten-Minute Tests book.

5 Column addition and subtraction

In the 11+ test, you need to be able to accurately use the formal written methods for addition and subtraction.

Before you begin

Column addition

83 738 + 15 472

```
   83738        83738        83738        83738
+  15472     +  15472     +  15472     +  15472
_____      _____      _____      _____
       0         1 0          210        99210
    1             1 1         1 1 1        1 1 1
```

1 Subtract the ones: 2 − 1 = 1. Write 1 in the ones column.

2 If you subtract 9 from 7, you get a minus number. Instead, borrow 1 from the hundreds column, making the hundreds column worth 3 and the tens column worth 17: 17 − 9 = 8 Write 8 in the tens column.

3 Subtract the hundreds, remembering you now only have 3 hundreds in the top row: 3 − 2 = 1 Write 1 in the hundreds column. Subtract the thousands: 8 − 7 = 1

4 Subtract the tens of thousands: 2 − 1 = 1 The answer is 11 181

1 Add the ones: 8 + 2 = 10. Write the zero in the ones column and carry the 1 over to under the tens column.

2 Add the tens, including the 1 carried over: 7 + 3 + 1 = 11. Write the 1 in the tens column and carry the 1 over to under the hundreds column.

3 Add the hundreds, including the 1 carried over: 7 + 4 + 1 = 12. Write the 2 in the hundreds column and carry the 1 to under the thousands column.

4 Add the thousands: 3 + 5 + 1 = 9. Write 9 in the thousands column.

5 Add the tens of thousands: 8 + 1 = 9. The answer is 99 210

Column subtraction

28 472 − 17 291

```
                      3 1              3 1
   28472           284̷7̷2           284̷7̷2
−  17291        −  17291        −  17291
_____         _____         _____
       1              81           11181
```

Worked examples

1 Ruby has 4569 stretchy bands and her friend Lucy has 2569 How many do they have altogether?

```
   4569
+ 2569
_____
   7138
  1 1 1
```

7138

1 9 + 9 = 18, so write 8 in the ones column and a 1 under the tens column.

2 6 + 6 + 1 = 13, so write 3 in the tens column and a 1 under the hundreds.

3 5 + 5 + 1 = 11, so write 1 in the hundreds column and a 1 under the thousands.

4 4 + 2 + 1 = 7, so there are 7 thousands.

2 Work out 8260 − 3109

```
       5 1
   82̷6̷0
−  3109
_____
   5151
```

5151

1 Subtracting 9 from 0 gives a negative number, so borrow a ten. The tens digit becomes 5

2 10 − 9 = 1. Write 1 in the ones column.

3 5 − 0 = 5. Write 5 in the tens column.

4 2 − 1 = 1. Write 1 in the hundreds column.

5 8 − 3 = 5. Write 5 in the thousands column.

Guided questions

1 Joe has bought a jumper costing £29.99 and some trousers costing £13.99

How much has he spent in total?

```
  £ 2 9 . 9 9
+ £ 1 3 . 9 9
  £ ☐☐ . 9 8
     1   1
```

You can add and subtract decimal numbers in the same way as whole numbers. Digits are written according to their place value and the decimal point is entered in the answer space as shown.

When dealing with money, use a £ symbol. If the answer has pence, write it with 2 decimal places to show the pounds to the left of the decimal point and pence to the right.

£ _____

2 Work out 26 828 + 13 457

```
  2 6 8 2 8
+ 1 3 4 5 7
  ☐☐☐ 8 5
       1
```

$8 + 7 = 15$ so write 1 under the tens column and 5 in the ones. $2 + 5 = 7$ plus the 1 underneath means there are 8 tens.

Write your answer on the line.

_____

3 Work out 25 846 – 12 475

```
  2 5 ⁷8̷ ¹4 6
- 1 2 4 7 5
  ☐☐☐ 7 1
```

$4 - 7$ gives a negative number, so you need to borrow one from the hundreds column instead and make it $14 - 7 = 7$
The hundreds digit in the top row becomes 7

Write your answer on the line.

_____

4 An apple farm has 63 170 sacks of apples in stock in the morning. In the afternoon, 29 466 are dispatched. How many sacks of apples are left in stock?

```
  6 3 1 7 0
- ☐☐☐☐☐
```

'Dispatched' means the apples were sent out for delivery, so you need to subtract to solve this problem.

_____

5 Complete this calculation.

```
  9 2 ¹2 ¹²3̷ ¹2
-   3 3 5 4 7
  ☐☐☐ 8 5
```

This calculation involves a lot of borrowing. Work methodically so that you don't get confused.

_____

6 Ben has £20. He buys a torch for £12.95 and a pair of gloves for £2.39

How much change does he get?

```
  £ 1 2 . 9 5        £ 2 0 . 0 0
+ £ 0 2 . 3 9      - £ ☐☐ . ☐☐
  £ 1 5 . 3 4
     1   1
```

This is a two-step problem. The first part has been done for you. You need to calculate the change by subtracting.

£ _____

Beyond the exam

Look at a shopping catalogue or a shopping website. Choose three items you would like to buy. Add up the prices to see how much money you would need. Check your answers with a calculator to see how accurate your written method is.

Have a go

1 What is the total of 2748 and 1875?

Write your digits in the correct columns.

1 mark

_____

2 Find the difference between 3562 and 2789

Think about the word 'difference' and whether you need to add or subtract.

1 mark

_____

3 Add together these two numbers:
   Thirty thousand, three hundred and twenty-three
   Twenty thousand, five hundred and five

Use place value to write the calculation correctly

1 mark

_____

4 A library has 34 567 non-fiction books. There are 3456 more fiction books than non-fiction. How many books does the library have altogether?

1 mark

_____

5 A theme park can admit 13 500 visitors a day. By midday, they can only allow 567 more people in. How many visitors were admitted in the morning?

Be careful when borrowing in subtraction calculations.

1 mark

_____

Time to reflect

Mark your _Have a go_ section out of 5. How are you doing so far?

Check your answers in the back of the book and see how you are doing.

Had a go	**Nearly there**	**Nailed it!**
0–2 marks	_3–4 marks_	_5 marks_
Have another look at the _Worked examples_ on page 24. Then try these questions again.	Look at your incorrect answers. Make sure you understand how to get the correct answer.	Congratulations! Now see whether you can get full marks on the _Timed practice_.

When you are ready, try the _Timed practice_ on the next page.

Timed practice

10

1 Add these four numbers together. Give your answer in digits.

Six thousand   three hundred and forty-eight   eight thousand   seven hundred

_____

| 1 |
| mark |

2 Find the difference between 9867 and 1003

_____

| 1 |
| mark |

3 A car costs £25 239 when new. It is sold 3 years later for £13 499
How much less is it worth at 3 years old?

£ _____

| 1 |
| mark |

4 There are thirty-four thousand and nine football fans at a match. Two thousand, three hundred and one leave at half time. How many stay? Give your answer in digits.

_____

| 1 |
| mark |

5 Clare has £1500 in her bank account. She spends £139.62 booking flights for her holiday and £482 booking a hotel. How much money does she have left?

£ _____

| 1 |
| mark |

6 This table shows the numbers of pupils at four schools.

School	Number of pupils
St Kevin's Primary	1431
Bluebell Hill Primary	102
Garden Lane School	1235
Redcoats Academy	843

a Calculate the difference between numbers of pupils in the largest and smallest schools.

_____

b Calculate the total number of pupils at the two largest schools.

_____

| 2 |
| marks |

Time to reflect

Mark your *Timed practice* section out of 7. How did you do?
Check your answers in the back of the book and write your score in the progress chart.

☐ *0–5 marks*
Scan the QR code for extra practice.
Then move on to the next practice section or try Test 5 in the Ten-Minute Tests book.

☐ *6–7 marks*
Well done! Move on to the next practice section or try Test 5 in the Ten-Minute Tests book.

6 Multiplication

In the 11+ test, you will need to be able to multiply using mental and written methods. You could be asked to find the product of decimals, whole numbers and multiples of 10, 100 and 1000

Before you begin

Mental methods
Times tables can be used to work out calculations such as: $60 \times 4 = 240$

$6 \times 4 = 24$, so $60 \times 4 = 24 \times 10 = 240$

123 Use **place value** to multiply numbers by **10, 100 and 1000**

1 To multiply by 10, move all digits 1 place to the left.

2 To multiply by 100, move all digits 2 place to the left.

3 To multiply by 1000, move all digits 3 places to the left.

Written methods
Use column multiplication to solve problems that are difficult to do mentally.

```
   4623
×     6
 27738
   3 1 1
```

Each digit in the large number has been multiplied by 6. Digits are carried in the same way as with written addition.

123 Short multiplication: This method is for **multiplying by one-digit numbers**.

```
    1           1           1           1
  582        582        582        582        582
×  32      ×  32      ×  32      ×  32      ×  32
   60        460      17460      17460      17460
                                + 1164       1164
                                            18624
                                              1
```

123 Long multiplication: This method is for multiplying by numbers with **more than one** digit.

1 Multiply each digit of the larger number by 30, so start the working with $30 \times 2 = 60$

2 $30 \times 80 = 2400$. Carry the 2 over to the thousands column.

3 $30 \times 500 = 15000$. Add the carried over 2 to get 17

4 Multiply each digit of the larger number by 2 (as for short multiplication).

5 Add together the two numbers to get the total answer.

123 Writing numbers in the correct place value columns is very important for accuracy. You can multiply decimals in the same way as whole numbers, but make sure you position the decimal point carefully.

Worked examples

1 Multiply 0.7 by 1000

$0.7 \times 1000 = \underline{\hspace{2em} 700 \hspace{2em}}$

Each digit has been moved 3 places to the left.

2 Alfie has 25 boxes of pencils. Each box contains 125 pencils. How many pencils does Alfie have in total?

```
   1 2
   125
×   25
  2500
   625
  3125
  1
```

$\underline{\hspace{2em} 3125 \hspace{2em}}$

Long multiplication has been used because you need to multiply by a 2-digit number.

The digits are multiplied by a **multiple of ten**, so the answer will end in a zero, for example: $20 \times 5 = 100$

You can use the multiplication fact $6 \times 7 = 42$ to help you.

3 What is the product of 0.6 and 0.7?

$0.6 \times 0.7 = 0.42$

$\underline{\hspace{2em} 0.42 \hspace{2em}}$

123 'Product' means the result of multiplying.

Guided questions

1 Circle the calculation with the largest product.

A 700 × 300   B 70 × 300   C 7000 × 3   D ~~0.7 × 3000~~

> Work out all of the multiplications and compare the answers.

2 Complete the table by multiplying the numbers by 10, 100 and 1000

Number	× 10	× 100	× 1000
0.26	2.6	a _____	260
357	b _____	35 700	357 000
9.15	91.5	915	c _____

> Use place value to move each digit by either 1, 2 or 3 places.

> Each digit has been moved 2 places because you are multiplying by 100

3 How much will it cost for 5 children and 1 adult to go to the soft play centre?

	Cost
Adult	Free
Child	£4.99

$$£ \overset{4}{4} . \overset{4}{9} \ 9$$
$$\times \qquad\quad 5$$
$$£ \ \square\square . 9 \ 5$$

£ _____

> **123** When calculating with amounts of money, remember to use two decimal places.

4 Use the function machine to multiply these numbers.

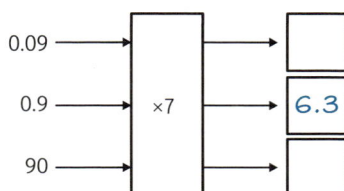

0.09 →
0.9 → ×7 → 6.3
90 →

> You can use the multiplication fact 9 × 7 = 63 here. 0.9 × 7 gives a result ten times smaller than 63

5 Complete the calculation.

$$\begin{array}{r} 6\ 7\ 2\ 5 \\ \times \qquad 7\ 2 \\ \hline \square\square\square\square\square\ 0 \\ \square\square\square\ 5\ 0 \\ \hline \square\square\square\square\square\ 0 \end{array}$$

> The third answer line is where you add the other two totals together.

6 Charlotte has 60 marbles. Her friend Vincent has 5 times this amount. How many marbles does Vincent have?

> You can use the multiplication fact 6 × 5 to calculate this mentally.

_____

Beyond the exam

Use your mental calculation skills to estimate the answer to each of these multiplications. Spend no more than 10 seconds estimating each answer.

332 × 17   4028 × 8   196 × 11   2123 × 13

Now use a written method to work out each calculation. How accurate were your estimates?

Have a go

1 Work out each calculation.

> Use your knowledge of place value to multiply these numbers.

a $12 \times 100 =$ _____

b $0.6 \times 1000 =$ _____

c $6.3 \times 10 =$ _____

d $460 \times 100 =$ _____

4 marks

2 Multiply these numbers together.

> Use the times tables to help you.

a $3 \times 6 =$ _____

b $0.3 \times 6 =$ _____

c $30 \times 6 =$ _____

d $300 \times 6 =$ _____

4 marks

3 A pack of cups costs £3.25
Mr Smith buys 100 packs for an event. How much does he spend?

> Use place value to multiply.

1 mark

£ _____

4 A theatre sells 620 tickets per day. How many did they sell in two weeks?

> Use long multiplication to solve this.

1 mark

_____

5 Keith thinks of a number. He multiplies it by 10 and then 100
His answer is 712
What number did he start with?

> Write down the steps and work backwards to answer this question.

1 mark

_____

6 If $145 \times 3 = 435$, what is 290×3?

> 290 is double 145

1 mark

_____

Time to reflect

Mark your *Have a go* section out of 12. How are you doing so far?

Check your answers in the back of the book and see how you are doing.

Had a go	**Nearly there**	**Nailed it!**
0–5 marks	*6–11 marks*	*12 marks*
Have another look at the *Worked examples* on page 28. Then try these questions again.	Look at your incorrect answers. Make sure you understand how to get the correct answer.	Congratulations! Now see whether you can get full marks on the *Timed practice*.

When you are ready, try the *Timed practice* on the next page.

Timed practice

⏱ **10**

1 What is 136×15?

_____

1 mark

2 Circle the correct statement.

$213 \times 10 = 2.13$

$213 \times 100 = 2130$

$213 \times 1000 = 213\,000$

$21.3 \times 100 = 21\,300$

1 mark

3 Bags of crisps cost £0.36 and Steve buys 5 bags. How much does he pay?

£ _____

1 mark

4 $4560 = 45.60 \times$ _____

Circle the missing number in the calculation.

10   100   1000   0.1

1 mark

5 What is 6451×27?

_____

1 mark

6 One box of chocolates costs £2.46

How much will 32 boxes cost?

£ _____

1 mark

7 What is 6.3×1.2? Circle the correct answer.

7.56   7.84   7.64   7.65

1 mark

Time to reflect

Mark your _Timed practice_ section out of 7. How did you do?

Check your answers in the back of the book and write your score in the progress chart.

☐ *0–5 marks*
Scan the QR code for extra practice.
Then move on to the next practice section or
try Test 6 in the Ten-Minute Tests book.

☐ *6–7 marks*
Well done!
Move on to the next practice section or try
Test 6 in the Ten-Minute Tests book.

7 Division

In the 11+ test, you may be asked to do written and mental calculations involving division.

Before you begin

Mental division

You can use known times tables facts to divide mentally. For example, you know that 9×7 is 63, so $63 \div 9 = 7$

You can also use **place value** to **divide by 10, 100 and 1000**

÷ 10	move all digits 1 place to the right
÷ 100	move all digits 2 places to the right
÷ 1000	move all digits 3 places to the right

123 **Division** means to split a numbers into equal groups. Each number in the calculation has a name:

In the calculation $12 \div 3 = 4$,

- 12 is the **dividend**.
- 3 is the **divisor**.
- 4 is the **quotient**.

Written division

You can use **short division** when the divisor is 12 or less, because you know times tables facts.

Long division is used for **larger divisors**, and it involves more steps.

Remainders

Remainders are the amounts left over after a number has been divided into equal parts. You can present these very simply in three ways:

- As a remainder: $23 \div 4 = 5$ r3
- As a fraction of the divisor: $5\frac{3}{4}$
- As a decimal: 5.75

Worked examples

1 a Calculate $9363 \div 11$

Step 1

$11\overline{)9\,^93\,6\,3}$

$9 \div 11 = 0$

Step 2

$11\overline{)9\,^93\,^56\,3}$

$93 \div 11 = 8$ r 5

Step 3

$11\overline{)9\,^93\,^56\,^13}$

$56 \div 11 = 5$ r 1

Step 4

$11\overline{)9\,^93\,^56\,^13}$

$13 \div 11 = 1$ r 2

$851\frac{2}{11}$

① $9 \div 11$ is less than 1, so carry the 9 over.

② $93 \div 11 = 8$ with 5 left over, so carry the 5 over.

③ $56 \div 11 = 5$ with 1 left over, so carry the 1 over.

④ $13 \div 11 = 1$ with 2 left over. You write this as 'r2' (remainder 2).

b Calculate $4972 \div 23$

Step 1

$23\overline{)4\,9\,7\,2}$

$216\frac{4}{23}$

Step 2

$23\overline{)4\,9\,7\,2}$
$4\,6\,0\,0$ 23 × 200
$3\,7\,2$

Step 3

$23\overline{)4\,9\,7\,2}$
$4\,6\,0\,0$ 23 × 200
$3\,7\,2$
$2\,3\,0$ 23 × 10
$1\,4\,2$

Step 4

$23\overline{)4\,9\,7\,2}$ 2 1 6 r 4
$4\,6\,0\,0$ 23 × 200
$3\,7\,2$
$2\,3\,0$ 23 × 10
$1\,4\,2$
$1\,3\,8$ 23 × 6
4

It might help you to write out multiples of the divisor before you start. Multiples of 23 which might help you are: 23, 46, 69, 92, 115, 138

$4 \div 23$ is less than 1, so there is nothing to write in the thousands column on the top answer line.

$49 \div 23 = 2$ r3 Subtract 4600 (23 × 200) from 4972 leaving 372 Write 2 in the hundreds column on the top answer line.

$37 \div 23 = 1$ r14 Subtract 230 (23 × 10) from 372 leaving 142 Write 1 in the tens column on the top answer line.

$142 \div 23 = 6$ r4 (Use the multiples list.) Subtract 138 (23 × 6) from 142 and write 6 on the top answer line. Then write 4 as a remainder on the top answer line.

Guided questions

1 Complete these calculations.

a $96 \div 6 =$ _____

b $124 \div 4 =$ _____

c $3.2 \div 8 =$ _____0.4_____

> Use multiplication facts to work out these calculations.

2 Divide each number by 10, 100 and 1000 to complete the diagram.

	÷10	÷100	÷1000
260	26	**a** ___2.6___	0.26
3	**b** _____	0.03	0.003
9651	965.1	96.51	**c** _____

> Remember that you move digits to the **right** by 1, 2, or 3 spaces when dividing by 10, 100 and 1000

3 Circle the **two** correct answers to $228 \div 8$ •

28   $28\frac{4}{8}$ 28 r4   28.4   28 r2

> Use a written method to find the answer. Compare your answers to the options above.

> 28.4 is not the same as 28 r4

4 A factory worker needs to pack 726 pencils into boxes.
Each box holds 15 pencils. How many whole boxes will they fill?

```
        4 □ r □
  15 | 7  2  6
      6  0  0
      □□□
      □□□
       □
```

> There are four 15s in 72 with 12 left over.
> Subtract 15×40 from 726 to find how many 15s are in this number.

5 Calculate $69.3 \div 2$ •

_____

> Use long division for this question. Add a 0 after the 3 and carry the 1 to get 10

6 Year 3 is going on a school trip. There are 53 children and 6 members of staff. How many 9-seater minibuses do they need?

_____

1 The dividend will be $53 + 6 = 59$. This is because there are 59 people travelling.

2 The divisor will be 9, as each minibus carries 9 people, so you need to split 59 into 9 equal shares.

3 The times tables fact $9 \times 6 = 54$ helps here: $59 \div 9 = 6$ r5 or $6\frac{5}{9}$

4 You cannot hire a fraction of a minibus, so round up to the nearest whole number.

Have a go

1 Circle the answer to the calculation.

1 mark

$47.2 \div 10$

4.72   472   0.472   47.02

2 Work out $6784 \div 9$

> Short division is useful for one-digit divisors.

1 mark

_____

3 $630 \div 7 =$ _____

1 mark

> Use the seven times table to help you.

4 Complete the calculations.

a $789 \div$ _____ $= 7.89$

b $6.2 \div$ _____ $= 0.62$

3 marks

c $56\,987 \div$ _____ $= 56.987$

> Digits move to the right when you divide a number by 10, 100 or 1000

5 $897 \div 13$

> Use long division when the divisor is greater than 12

1 mark

_____

6 The population of Megaville is 10 times larger than that of Midtown. The population of Littleburg is 10 times smaller than that of Midtown. If the population of Megaville is 310 000, what is the population of Littleburg?

1 mark

_____

Time to reflect

Mark your *Have a go* section out of 8. How are you doing so far?

Check your answers in the back of the book and see how you are doing.

Had a go
0–5 marks
Have another look at the *Worked examples* on page 32. Then try these questions again.

Nearly there
6–7 marks
Look at your incorrect answers. Make sure you understand how to get the correct answer.

Nailed it!
8 marks
Congratulations! Now see whether you can get full marks on the *Timed practice*.

When you are ready, try the *Timed practice* on the next page.

Timed practice

⏱ **10**

1 Calculate $5678 \div 6$

Give your answer as a whole number and a remainder.

_____

1 mark

2 Divide these numbers.

a $456 \div 10 =$ _____

b $63.25 \div 100 =$ _____

c $98\,564 \div 1000 =$ _____

d $500.1 \div 100 =$ _____

4 marks

3 George pays £96 for 24 pots of paint. Each pot costs the same amount.

How much does each paint pot cost?

£ _____

1 mark

4 $999 \div 3 =$ _____

1 mark

5 Mr Gallagher is setting out chairs for an assembly. Each row contains 8 chairs, and there are 163 chairs in total. How many complete rows of chairs can he make?

_____

1 mark

6 George has 128 paintings to display. He wants to arrange them in rows with an equal number of paintings in each one. Circle the number of paintings he should put in each row.

3   4   5   6   7

1 mark

7 A sweet shop owner has a jar of 268 jelly beans, which she shares equally into 14 individual bags. Complete the sentence.

There are _____ sweets in each bag with _____ left over.

1 mark

Time to reflect

Mark your *Timed practice* section out of 10. How did you do?
Check your answers in the back of the book and write your score in the progress chart.

☐ **0–8 marks**
Scan the QR code for extra practice.
Then move on to the next practice section or try Test 7 in the Ten-Minute Tests book.

☐ **9–10 marks**
Well done!
Move on to the next practice section or try Test 7 in the Ten-Minute Tests book.

Checkpoint 1

In this checkpoint, you will practise skills from the **Number** and **Calculation** topics. There are 16 questions for you to answer.

(15)

1 mark

1 Circle the number with the lowest value.

89 001   89 010   89 100   89 110

→ Section 1

1 mark

2 Write these numbers in order, starting with the lowest.

45 036   4536   450 036   45 630

_____   _____   _____   _____

→ Section 1

3 marks

3 Complete the table by rounding these numbers as shown.

→ Section 1

Number	Nearest 10	Nearest 100	Nearest 1000
75 562	75 560	b _____	76 000
12 002	12 000	12 000	c _____
9987	a _____	10 000	10 000

1 mark

4 On Monday, the temperature is −2 °C. On Tuesday, it is 3 degrees warmer than it was on Monday. Circle Tuesday's temperature.

−5 °C   −1 °C   1 °C   0 °C

→ Section 2

3 marks

5 Identify the missing temperatures.

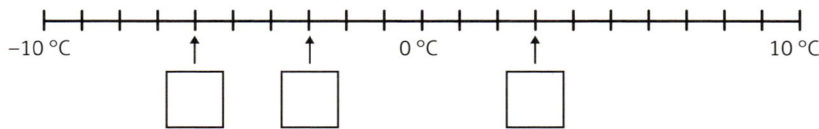

−10 °C   0 °C   10 °C

→ Section 2

3 marks

6 Complete the sequence.

0.05,   0.07,   0.09,   _____,   0.13,   _____,   _____

→ Section 3

3 marks

7 Round

a 7.95 to the nearest whole one   _____

b 0.015 to the nearest hundredth   _____

c 6.329 to the nearest tenth   _____

→ Section 1

8 Lucy, Peter and Darren had a competition to see which of them could jump the highest. The table shows their results.

→ Section 3

Name	Jump height in metres
Lucy	1.63
Peter	1.62
Darren	1.71

2 marks

a The winner was _____ .

b The person in 3rd place was _____ .

9 Write these Roman numerals in modern numbers.

 a MDCC = _____

 b LXXX = _____

Section 4

2 marks

10 Ben has 497 football cards and Stacy has 367. How many football cards do they have altogether?

_____

Section 5

1 mark

11 Work out 58 754 − 32 898

_____

Section 5

1 mark

12 Complete the chart.

Section 6

Number	× 10	× 100	× 1000
8.6	86	**a** _____	8600
5.63	**b** _____	563	**c** _____

3 marks

13 Tickets to see a play are £5.60 each. How much will five tickets cost?

£ _____

Section 6

1 mark

14 Work out 7523 × 23

_____

Section 6

1 mark

15 Work out 560 ÷ 7

_____

Section 7

1 mark

16 A farmer picks 578 apples. He wants to sell them in bags of 12
 How many whole bags of 12 apples can he make?

Section 7

_____

1 mark

Time to reflect

Mark your *Checkpoint* out of 28. How did you do?

1 Check your answers in the back of the book and write your score in the progress chart. If any of
 your answers are incorrect, use the section links to find out which practice sections to look at again.

2 Scan the QR code for extra practice.

3 Move on to the next practice section.

8 Fractions

In the 11+ test, you could be asked to simplify fractions or to find equivalent fractions. You could also be asked to convert between improper fractions and mixed numbers.

Before you begin

Equivalent fractions

Equivalent fractions have different numerators (top digit) and denominators (bottom digit), but their overall value is **equal**. Find equivalent fractions by multiplying or dividing the **numerator** and **denominator** by the **same** number.

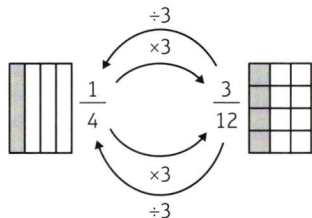

$\div 3$
$\times 3$
$\frac{1}{4}$
$\frac{3}{12}$
$\times 3$
$\div 3$

Both numbers are multiplied by (or divided by) 3 as it is the highest common factor of 12 and 3

You may be asked to **simplify** a fraction. Here, the simplest form is $\frac{1}{4}$ because you can't divide the numerator and denominator any further.

123 **Factors** are numbers which fit **exactly** into another number with no remainder. For example, 3 is a factor of 12 as it fits in exactly 4 times with no remainder. **Common factors** are shared by 2 or more numbers. The common factors of 12 and 8 are 2, 3 and 6

6 is the **highest common factor**.

Mixed numbers and improper fractions

Mixed numbers consist of a whole number and a fraction. They are always worth more than 1 whole.

Improper fractions have larger numerators than denominators. They are also worth more than 1 whole.

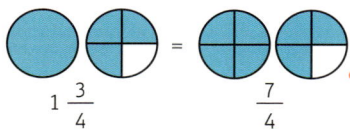

$1\frac{3}{4}$ = $\frac{7}{4}$

$\frac{7}{4}$ is an improper fraction. There are enough quarters to make 1 whole, with 3 quarters left over.

$1\frac{3}{4}$ is a mixed number. 1 whole contains 4 quarters,

so $1\frac{3}{4}$ is equal to $\frac{4}{4} + \frac{3}{4} = \frac{7}{4}$

Worked examples

1 Write down the equivalent fractions shown in this diagram.

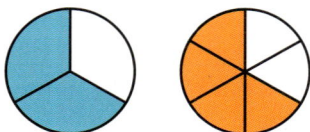

$\frac{2}{3}$ and $\frac{4}{6}$

There are 3 parts; 2 are shaded.

There are 6 parts; 4 are shaded.

2 Each rectangle is worth 1 whole. Write the shaded amount as a mixed number and then write it as an improper fraction.

Mixed number: $1\frac{4}{5}$ Improper fraction: $\frac{9}{5}$

There is 1 whole and 4 fifths.

There are 9 fifths. 5 fifths equal 1 whole.

Guided questions

1 Write the equivalent fractions shown in the diagrams.

> 3 is a common factor of 3 and 6

a

$$\frac{3}{6} = \frac{1}{2}$$

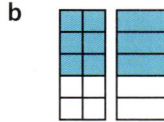

b

c

2 Write the missing numbers in these pairs of equivalent fractions.

a $\frac{3}{10} = \frac{30}{100}$ **b** $\frac{5}{8} = \frac{10}{\square}$

> The denominator and numerator must **both** be multiplied by 10, as $10 \times 10 = 100$

3 Convert these improper fractions into mixed numbers.

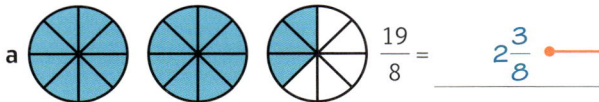

a $\frac{19}{8} = 2\frac{3}{8}$

> There are 19 eighths. $\frac{16}{8}$ makes 2 wholes with $\frac{3}{8}$ left over.

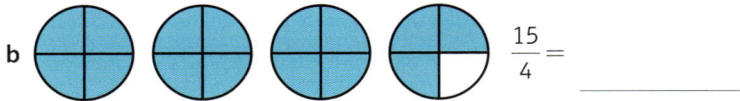

b $\frac{15}{4} =$

> To convert improper fractions to mixed numbers, divide the numerator by the denominator.

4 Circle the fraction equivalent to $\frac{4}{5}$

$\frac{8}{5}$ $\frac{4}{10}$ $\frac{8}{10}$

> Multiply or divide the numerator and denominator by the **same** number to find an equivalent.

5 Write these fractions in their simplest form.

a $\frac{4}{10} = \frac{2}{5}$ **b** $\frac{10}{100} =$

> Keep dividing both the numerator and denominator by common factors until you can't divide any further.

6 a Divide the circles below into thirds and shade in $1\frac{1}{3}$

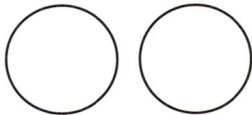

> It is unlikely that you'll be asked to draw fractions in the exam, but it can be a useful technique to help you visualise fractions while you are learning.

b Circle the fraction equivalent to $1\frac{1}{3}$

$\frac{5}{3}$ $\frac{4}{3}$ $\frac{2}{3}$

> **123** Remember that fractions are always **equal parts**. For example, splitting a shape into 4 equal parts will give you quarters.

Beyond the exam

Next time you bake something, try out a recipe that has fractional and mixed number measurements. Baking recipes often use fractions of teaspoon measures.

Have a go

2 marks

1   Fill in the missing numbers to make the fraction pairs equivalent.

a $\dfrac{7}{20} = \dfrac{}{100}$ b $\dfrac{5}{8} = \dfrac{15}{}$

1 mark

2   All but one of these fractions are equivalent. Circle the odd one out.

$\dfrac{5}{10}$ $\dfrac{6}{12}$ $\dfrac{5}{6}$ $\dfrac{15}{30}$ $\dfrac{2}{4}$

> Simplifying fractions allows you to compare them.

1 mark

3   What is $\dfrac{12}{48}$ in its simplest form? Circle the correct answer.

$\dfrac{6}{24}$ $\dfrac{24}{96}$ $\dfrac{1}{4}$ $\dfrac{2}{4}$ $\dfrac{3}{12}$

4   Complete the table by writing the equivalent mixed numbers and improper fractions for each diagram.

4 marks

	$1\dfrac{1}{4}$	$\dfrac{5}{4}$
	a _____	b _____
	c _____	d _____

3 marks

5   Write the equivalent improper fraction for each mixed number.

a $3\dfrac{4}{5} =$ _____   b $2\dfrac{2}{6} =$ _____   c $4\dfrac{1}{2} =$ _____

3 marks

6   Write the improper fractions as mixed numbers.

a $\dfrac{5}{3} =$ _____   b $\dfrac{7}{2} =$ _____   c $\dfrac{9}{4} =$ _____

Time to reflect

Mark your *Have a go* section out of 14. How are you doing so far?

Check your answers in the back of the book and see how you are doing.

Had a go	**Nearly there**	**Nailed it!**
0–5 marks	*6–13 marks*	*14 marks*
Have another look at the *Worked examples* on page 38. Then try these questions again.	Look at your incorrect answers. Make sure you understand how to get the correct answer.	Congratulations! Now see whether you can get full marks on the *Timed practice*.

When you are ready, try the *Timed practice* on the next page.

Timed practice

10

1 Write down the letter of the shape which matches each fraction.

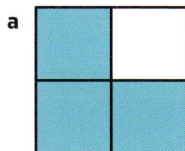

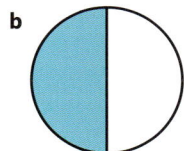

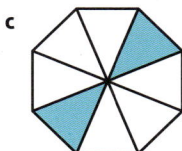

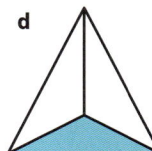

a   b   c   d

$\frac{5}{20}$ _____

$\frac{8}{16}$ _____

$\frac{20}{60}$ _____

$\frac{12}{16}$ _____

4 marks

2 Complete the table to show these fractions in their simplest form.

Fraction	Simplest form
$\frac{30}{100}$	a _____
$\frac{16}{32}$	b _____
$\frac{18}{81}$	c _____

3 marks

3 Circle the fraction that is not equivalent. $\frac{80}{100}$ $\frac{12}{15}$ $\frac{20}{24}$ $\frac{16}{20}$

1 mark

4 Emma cuts two pizzas into equal slices. She and her friend eat $1\frac{2}{4}$ of the pizzas. How much pizza do they have left over?

_____

1 mark

5 Complete the table to show the equivalent improper fractions and mixed numbers.

Mixed number	Improper fraction
$3\frac{1}{2}$	a _____
b _____	$\frac{6}{4}$
$5\frac{1}{10}$	c _____
$1\frac{3}{4}$	d _____
e _____	$\frac{9}{5}$

5 marks

Time to reflect

Mark your *Timed practice* section out of 14. How did you do?

Check your answers in the back of the book and write your score in the progress chart.

☐ *0–12 marks*
Scan the QR code for extra practice.
Then move on to the next practice section or try Test 8 in the Ten-Minute Tests book.

☐ *13–14 marks*
Well done!
Move on to the next practice section or try Test 8 in the Ten-Minute Tests book.

9 Percentages

In the 11+ test you need to understand what percentages are, know some common percentages and be able to find percentages of amounts.

Before you begin

Percentages

The word **percentage** means '**per one hundred**'. Percentages are used to show portions of amounts by **dividing** them into **100 equal parts**.

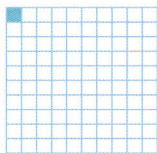

1 square out of 100 is $\frac{1}{100}$ or 1%.   10 squares out of 100 is $\frac{10}{100}$ or 10%.   25 squares out of 100 is $\frac{25}{100}$ or 25%.   50 squares out of 100 is $\frac{50}{100}$ or 50%.

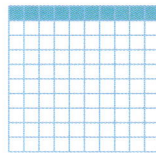

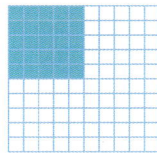

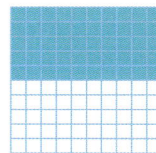

Percentages can be converted to fractions of 100. For example, 25% can be written as $\frac{25}{100}$

123 100% and $\frac{100}{100}$ are both the same as 1 whole.

123 Other percentages can be found using these percentages. To find 20% you could find 10% and **double** it.

Percentages of amounts

To find percentages of amounts, you can use mental calculations.

Percentage	Equivalent to	Calculation	Example: Percentage of 24
1%	$\frac{1}{100}$ or **one hundredth** of the number	÷ 100	$24 \div 100 = 0.24$
10%	$\frac{10}{100}$ or **one tenth** of the number	÷ 10	$24 \div 10 = 2.4$
25%	$\frac{25}{100}$ or **one quarter** of the number	÷ 4 (or halve then halve again)	$24 \div 4 = 6$
50%	$\frac{50}{100}$ or **half** of the number	÷ 2	$24 \div 2 = 12$
100%	$\frac{100}{100}$ or **all** of the number		24

Worked examples

1 What percentage of the hundred square is shaded?

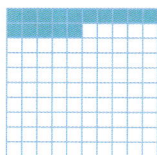

There are 100 small squares and 15 of them are shaded. 15 out of 100 is 15%.

_____15_____ %

2 David has 40 jelly sweets and gives 20% of them to Gina. How many jelly sweets does he have left?

_____32_____

1 Divide 40 by 10 to find 10% (4) and then double it to find 20% (8).

2 Then subtract 20% from the total number of jelly sweets to find out how many David has left ($40 - 8 = 32$).

Guided questions

1 What amount of each hundred square is shaded? Write your answers as a percentage and as a fraction.

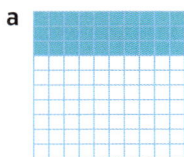

a

Percentage _____ 30 _____ %

Fraction $\dfrac{30}{100}$

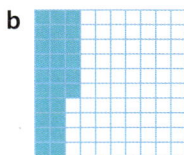

b

There are 26 squares shaded out of 100

Percentage _____ %

Fraction $\dfrac{\boxed{}}{100}$

2 What is 50% of 54?

_____

> To find 50%, divide by 2

3 Circle the number that is 30% of 300

30   90   3   9   500

> 10% of 300 = 30
> 3 lots of 10% will give the value of 30%.

4 A clothing shop has a sale. Apply the following discounts to find the sale prices.

a 25% discount to a shirt which costs £20 at full price = £ _____ 15 _____

b 10% discount to some trousers which cost £32 at full price = £ _____

c 20% discount to some shoes which cost £15 at full price = £ _____

> To find 25% divide by 4
> Subtract £5 from £20 to find the sale price of £15

> To find 10% divide by 10
> Subtract this from the full price.

> To find 20%, first find 10% and then double the discount. Subtract the discount from the original price to find the sale price.

5 Circle the calculation with the lowest value

25% of 200   75% of 40   10% of 800   15% of 60

> 25% of 40 = 10, so
> 75% = 10 × 3 = 30
> This is not the lowest value.

> To work out 15%, first find 10% and then find 5% by halving 10%. Finally, add the two amounts together.

> 10% sounds small, but 10% of 800 = 80
> This is actually the highest value.

6 Find 25% of 72

72 ÷ 2 = 36
36 ÷ 2 =

_____

> To find 25%, divide by 4 (or halve 72 and then halve the answer again).

Beyond the exam

Look for percentage discounts next time you go shopping. They are often 25%, 10% or 50%. Use mental calculations to work out how much money you would save.

Have a go

1 Write what percentages of these squares are shaded and unshaded.

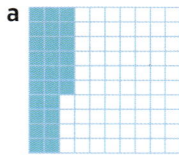

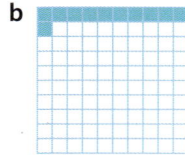

a

b

> Check that your percentages for the shaded and unshaded portions of the squares add up to 100

shaded = _____ %   shaded = _____ %

unshaded = _____ %   unshaded = _____ %

2 marks

2 Find 25% of 88

_____

> Finding 25% is the same as dividing by 4

1 mark

3 15% of the weight of a 300 g fruit cake is sugar. What is the weight of the sugar?

_____ g

> Finding 10% can help you calculate other percentages.

1 mark

4 Circle the calculation with the highest value.

25% of 400   10% of 600   15% of 500   20% of 300

> A larger percentage doesn't always mean a larger value. For example, 10% of 800 is more than 50% of 100

1 mark

5 Martine has a cake weighing 500 g. She cuts off 2 slices, each weighing 10% of the original weight. What does the remainder of the cake weigh in grams?

_____ g

1 mark

6 What percentage of this shape is unshaded?

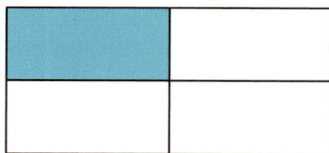

> Remember that half of a whole is worth 50%.

_____ %

1 mark

Time to reflect

Mark your *Have a go* section out of 7. How are you doing so far?

Check your answers in the back of the book and see how you are doing.

☐ **Had a go**	☐ **Nearly there**	☐ **Nailed it!**
0–3 marks	4–6 marks	7 marks
Have another look at the *Worked examples* on page 42. Then try these questions again.	Look at your incorrect answers. Make sure you understand how to get the correct answer.	Congratulations! Now see whether you can get full marks on the *Timed practice*.

When you are ready, try the *Timed practice* on the next page.

Timed practice

⏱ 10

1 Find 30% of 40

_____

1 mark

2 Find 60% of 30

_____

1 mark

3 Paul buys a pair of flip flops which originally cost £25. They are discounted by 30%. What does he pay for the flip flops?

£ _____

1 mark

4 Circle the true statement.

50% of 60 = 32   10% of 66 = 6.6   15% of 80 = 11

1 mark

5 Mrs Peters has a collection of 120 stamps.

30% of them are red, 25% are green and the rest are blue. How many blue stamps does she have?

_____

1 mark

6 Complete the chart below with percentages and fractions of £40

Amount of £40	Percentage	Fraction
£10	a _____ %	b $\dfrac{\boxed{}}{100}$
£8	c _____ %	d $\dfrac{\boxed{}}{100}$
£30	e _____ %	f $\dfrac{\boxed{}}{100}$

6 marks

Time to reflect

Mark your *Timed practice* section out of 11. How did you do?
Check your answers in the back of the book and write your score in the progress chart.

☐ *0–9 marks*
Scan the QR code for extra practice.
Then move on to the next practice section or try Test 9 in the Ten-Minute Tests book.

☐ *10–11 marks*
Well done!
Move on to the next practice section or try Test 9 in the Ten-Minute Tests book.

10 Equivalence

In the 11+ test you will need to be able to recall from memory and work out simple equivalent fractions, decimals and percentages.

Before you begin

Equivalence

Equivalent means **the same as**. You can convert between **percentages, decimals** and **fractions** using mental maths and place value.

Percentage	Fraction	Decimal
100%	$\frac{100}{100}$ or $\frac{1}{1}$ (1 whole)	1
75%	$\frac{75}{100}$ or $\frac{3}{4}$	0.75
50%	$\frac{50}{100}$ or $\frac{1}{2}$	0.5
25%	$\frac{25}{100}$ or $\frac{1}{4}$	0.25
20%	$\frac{20}{100}$ or $\frac{1}{5}$	0.2
10%	$\frac{10}{100}$ or $\frac{1}{10}$	0.1

123 Percent means **out of 100**, so you can easily write fractions and decimals as hundredths if you know the percentage.

The second column of the table shows the **decimal fraction** (out of 100) and the **simplified** fraction. Decimal fractions can be simplified by dividing by the **highest common factor** of the numerator and the denominator.

Worked examples

1 Show 35% as a fraction and a decimal.

Fraction: $\frac{35}{100}$ or $\frac{7}{20}$

Decimal: 0.35

35% means 35 out of 100, so write 35 as the numerator and 100 as the denominator. 5 is a common factor of 35 and 100, so simplify the fraction by dividing them both by 5

$35\% = \frac{35}{100}$. This decimal fraction can be written as 0.35 using place value.

2 Chloe hangs ten socks out to dry. 7 are black and the rest are grey. What percentage of the socks are grey?

30 %

① 7 out of 10 socks are black. This can be written as $\frac{7}{10}$, which is the same as $\frac{70}{100}$ or 70%.

② 3 socks must be grey. This can be written as $\frac{3}{10}$, which is the same as $\frac{30}{100}$ or 30%.

3 What percentage of this shape is not shaded?

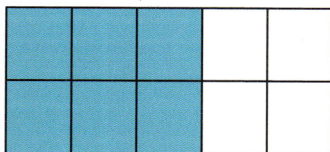

40 %

4 out of 10 squares are not shaded. $\frac{4}{10}$ is equivalent to $\frac{40}{100}$, which is the same as 40%.

Guided questions

1 Complete the table by filling in the missing percentages, fractions and decimals.

Percentage	Decimal fraction	Simplified fraction	Decimal
55%	$\frac{55}{100}$	$\frac{11}{20}$	0.55
15%	$\frac{15}{100}$	**a** _____	0.15
b _____	$\frac{5}{100}$	$\frac{1}{20}$	0.05
80%	$\frac{80}{100}$	$\frac{8}{10}$	**c** _____

> 15% means 15 out of 100
> Simplify this fraction using the common factor 5

> Convert decimals to % by multiplying by 100
> For example, $0.05 \times 100 = 5$

> 80% is the same as 80 hundredths. Use place value to write this as a decimal.

2 Harry drinks 75% of his bottle of juice. What fraction of the juice does he have left?

_____

> 75% is equivalent to $\frac{75}{100}$. 25% is left.

3 Circle the calculation with the highest value.

50% of 68 $\frac{1}{4}$ of 100 0.5×80 10% of 200

> This has the **lowest** value as 10% of 200 is 20

> This is **not** the highest value as $\frac{1}{4}$ of 100 is 25

4 Chris has a large chocolate cake in his café. He cuts it into 20 slices and sells 12 of the slices by lunch time. What percentage of the cake is left for afternoon tea?

_____ %

> Chris sells $\frac{12}{20}$. You can also multiply the numerator and denominator by 5 to write it as $\frac{60}{100}$. This makes it easier to work out the percentage.

5 Circle the incorrect statement.

35% = 0.35 $\frac{1}{5} = 25\%$ $\frac{1}{4} = 0.25$ 0.65 = 65%

> 0.25 is **equivalent** to $\frac{25}{100}$, which **simplifies** to $\frac{1}{4}$

Beyond the exam

Make a set of number cards showing the following fractions:

$\frac{21}{56}$ $\frac{1}{2}$ $\frac{49}{98}$ $\frac{2}{3}$ $\frac{3}{8}$ $\frac{23}{36}$ $\frac{4}{7}$ $\frac{16}{42}$ $\frac{28}{49}$ $\frac{8}{21}$

Shuffle the cards and play snap with a friend. Take turns to turn over a card so you can both see it. If it is equivalent to the previous card, shout 'Snap!'

Have a go

1 Circle the values equivalent to 10%.

2 marks

0.01   0.1   10.0 $\frac{1}{10}$ $\frac{10}{10}$ $\frac{10}{50}$

> Remember, $100\% = 1 = \frac{100}{100}$

2 Jill walks two tenths of 150 km. Circle the equivalent value.

1 mark

25%   2%   0.02   0.2   10%

> Converting fractions to hundredths can help you to find equivalent decimals and percentages.

3 Write the missing values on the number line.

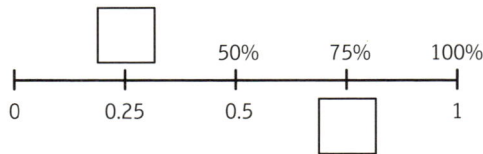

2 marks

| □ | 50% | 75% | 100% |

0   0.25   0.5   □   1

> Convert decimals to percentages by multiplying by 100%.

4 Write these values in order, starting with the highest.

1 mark

75%   0.90 $\frac{8}{10}$ 0.89

_____   _____   _____   _____

> Writing all the values in the same form (percentage, decimal or fraction) will make them easier to compare.

5 Class 5 carry out a survey of pets. Out of 30 children, 10% have rabbits, $\frac{1}{2}$ have cats and the rest have dogs. How many children have dogs?

1 mark

_____

> Calculate the known values first.

Time to reflect

Mark your *Have a go* section out of 7. How are you doing so far?

Check your answers in the back of the book and see how you are doing.

Had a go	**Nearly there**	**Nailed it!**
0–3 marks	*4–6 marks*	*7 marks*
Have another look at the *Worked examples* on page 46. Then try these questions again.	Look at your incorrect answers. Make sure you understand how to get the correct answer.	Congratulations! Now see whether you can get full marks on the *Timed practice*.

When you are ready, try the *Timed practice* on the next page.

Timed practice

10

1 Complete the table.

Fraction	Decimal	Percentage
$\frac{6}{10}$	**a** _____	60%
$\frac{78}{100}$	0.78	**b** _____ %
c _____	0.21	**d** _____ %

4 marks

2 Circle the two equivalent values.

0.65 $\frac{7}{10}$ 20%   70%

2 marks

3 Write the fraction, decimal and percentage of the whole grid that is shaded.

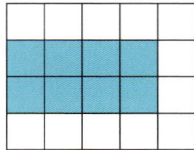

Fraction = _____

Decimal = _____

Percentage = _____

3 marks

4 Place these values in order, from lowest to highest.

10% of 55   0.6 × 50 $\frac{2}{10}$ of 30

_____   _____   _____

1 mark

5 Jake grows vegetables. 15% of his vegetable patch is used for carrots and $\frac{3}{5}$ are used for potatoes.

The rest is used for onions. What percentage of the vegetable patch is left for growing onions?

_____ %

1 mark

6 Class 4 carried out a survey of the ways in which they travel to school.

Transport	Number of pupils
Bus	2
Cycle	3
Walk	15
Car	5

What percentage of Class 4 travel to school in a car?

_____ %

1 mark

Time to reflect

Mark your *Timed practice* section out of 12. How did you do?

Check your answers in the back of the book and write your score in the progress chart.

☐ *0–10 marks*
Scan the QR code for extra practice.
Then, move on to the next practice section or
try Test 10 in the Ten-Minute Tests book.

☐ *11–12 marks*
Well done!
Move on to the next practice section or try
Test 10 in the Ten-Minute Tests book.

11 Ratio and proportion

In the 11+ test, you might be asked to use ratio to divide quantities or to solve problems involving quantities. You'll need to be able to write ratios correctly using the : symbol and know how to simplify them.

Before you begin

Expressing ratios

Ratios are used to compare two or more amounts.

$\frac{3}{8}$ of the pizza is uneaten. $\frac{5}{8}$ of the pizza has been eaten.

The ratio of uneaten pizza to eaten pizza is 3:5

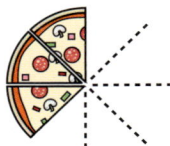

> Notice that the numbers in the ratio add up to the number of slices in the **whole** pizza.

You can **simplify** ratios in a similar way to fractions using **highest common factors**.

- 2:8 becomes 1:4 using the highest common factor 2
- 21:6 becomes 7:2 using the highest common factor 3

Sharing amounts using ratio

Amounts can be **shared** using ratios as shown in the steps below.

£100 is being shared between 2 friends using a ratio of 8:2

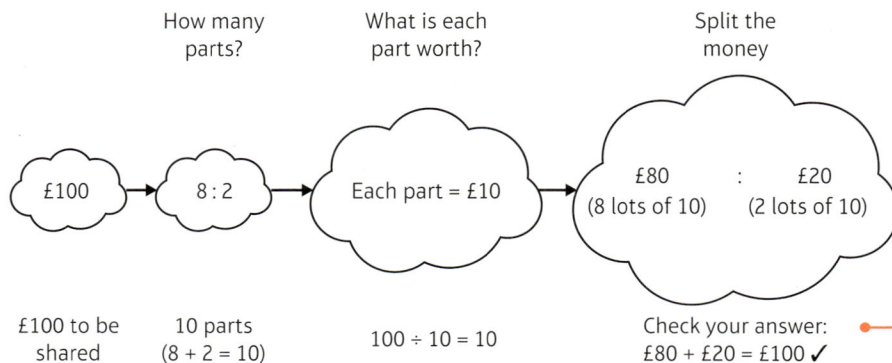

How many parts?	What is each part worth?	Split the money

£100 → 8:2 → Each part = £10 → £80 : £20
(8 lots of 10) (2 lots of 10)

£100 to be shared   10 parts (8 + 2 = 10)   100 ÷ 10 = 10   Check your answer: £80 + £20 = £100 ✓

> Always check that the shares add up to make the original amount.

Worked examples

1 On a school trip, there are 25 children and 10 adults. Write the ratio of children to adults in its simplest form.

25 children : 10 adults

> You are asked to find the ratio of **children to adults** so write the number of children **first**.

25 : 10

> Simplify the ratio by using common factors. 5 is the **highest common factor** of 25 and 10

5 : 2

> 25 ÷ 5 = 5 and 10 ÷ 5 = 2

2 Jafar and Millie want to share 96 apples using a ratio of 2:1. Jafar will get the larger share. How many apples will they each get?

Jafar gets _____64_____

> A ratio of 2:1 means that there are 3 parts **altogether**. 96 ÷ 3 = 32 so one part is worth 32 and 2 parts are worth 64

Millie gets _____32_____

> Check your answer. 64 + 32 = 96 which is correct as there are 96 apples in total.

Guided questions

1 What is the ratio of shaded to unshaded sections in the following shapes? Give your answers in their simplest form.

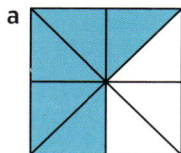

a

b

c

_____ 5 : 3 _____

_____ 1 : 3 _____

_____

> There are 5 shaded parts and 3 non-shaded parts, and 8 parts in **total**.

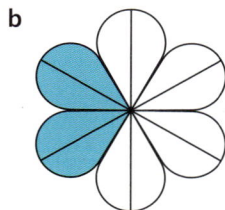

> There are 4 shaded to 8 non-shaded parts, giving a ratio of 4 : 8 **Simplify** this using the **HCF** 4 to give 1 : 3

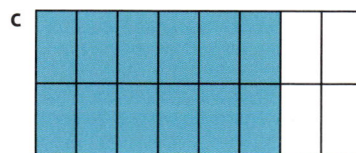

> There are 12 shaded parts and 4 non-shaded parts. Simplify 12 : 4 using the **common factor** 4

2 Complete the table by sharing 48 into the following ratios.

Ratio	Shares		
5 : 1	**a** ___40___	and	___8___
3 : 5	**b** ___18___	and	___30___
1 : 2	**c** _____	and	_____

> There are 6 parts. 48 ÷ 6 = 8, so each part is worth 8
> 5 parts = 40 and 1 part = 8

> There are 8 parts. 48 ÷ 8 = 6, so each part is worth 6
> 3 parts = 18 and 5 parts = 30

3 Dhruv wants to tile his bathroom in stripes of this pattern.

a What is the ratio of **white to blue** tiles? Give your answer in its simplest form.

> Ensure you put the numbers in the correct order.

_____

b Dhruv works out that he needs 18 blue tiles. How many white tiles will be needed to complete the pattern?

_____

> Make the numbers in a ratio larger by multiplying both numbers by the same amount.

Beyond the exam

Think about how many boys and girls there are in your class at school. Work out the ratio of boys to girls, giving your answer in its simplest form.

Have a go

1 James has a bag of marbles which contains six red marbles and nine blue marbles. What is the ratio of red to blue marbles? Give your answer in its simplest form.

> Use common factors to simplify.

1 mark

_____

2 Abigail is counting her pens. She has 16 metallic ones and 4 fluorescent ones. What is the ratio of fluorescent to metallic pens? Give your answer in its simplest form.

> Read the question carefully and make sure to write the numbers in the correct order.

1 mark

_____

3 Kate builds 3 toy cars every 2 hours. She builds cars for a total of 24 hours over the course of one week. How many toy cars does she make in that week?

> This can be done in stages. First work out how many cars she makes in 4 hours, then in 8, and so on.

1 mark

_____

4 Divide 24 into the following ratios:

a 1:5 _____

b 1:3 _____

3 marks

c 8:4 _____

5 Dylan has a recipe for 12 scones which calls for 100 g sugar. How much sugar will he need for 36 scones?

1 mark

_____ g

Time to reflect

Mark your *Have a go* section out of 7. How are you doing so far?

Check your answers in the back of the book and see how you are doing.

Had a go
0–4 marks
Have another look at the *Worked examples* on page 50. Then try these questions again.

Nearly there
5–6 marks
Look at your incorrect answers. Make sure you understand how to get the correct answer.

Nailed it!
7 marks
Congratulations! Now see whether you can get full marks on the *Timed practice*.

When you are ready, try the *Timed practice* on the next page.

Timed practice

10

1 Melissa is looking at some gerbils in a pet shop. 16 are white and 14 are brown. What is the ratio of white gerbils to brown gerbils in its simplest form?

_____

1 mark

2 Nazir is counting the fish in his fish tank. He has 11 stripy fish. He has 5 more spotty fish than stripy fish. What is the ratio of spotty to stripy fish?

_____

1 mark

3 Sarah and Carla are going to share 25 apples. For every 3 apples Sarah gets, Carla will get 2 apples.

How many apples does each person get?

Sarah gets _____

Carla gets _____

2 marks

4 In a car park, there are 3 red cars for every 6 blue cars. There are 18 blue cars. How many red cars are there?

_____

1 mark

5 The school cook makes a chocolate orange cake. The recipe calls for 5 teaspoons of orange flavouring to every 100 grams of cocoa. If the cook uses 15 teaspoons of orange flavouring, how many grams of cocoa must she use?

_____ g

1 mark

6 In one football season, the ratio of wins to losses for Southam United is 7:3
If they won 42 matches, how many did they lose?

_____

1 mark

Time to reflect

Mark your *Timed practice* section out of 7. How did you do?
Check your answers in the back of the book and write your score in the progress chart.

☐ *0—5 marks*
Scan the QR code for extra practice.
Then, move on to the next practice section or try Test 11 in the Ten-Minute Tests book.

☐ *6—7 marks*
Well done!
Move on to the next practice section or try Test 11 in the Ten-Minute Tests book.

12 Scale factors

In the 11+ test, you might be expected to use a scale factor to enlarge a shape. You also need to recognise what scale factor has been used when a shape has been enlarged, calculating new measurements by multiplying or dividing.

Before you begin

Scale factors

Scale factors are used to describe **enlargements** of shapes. When a shape is enlarged, **all** its measurements are increased or decreased in the **same** ratio. The angle sizes of the shape remain unchanged. You can describe the original shape and the enlarged shape as **similar**.

You may be asked to identify what **scale factor** has been used to **enlarge** a shape.

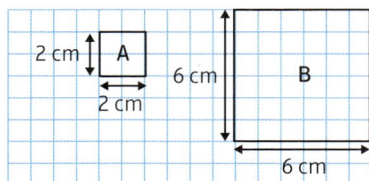

All the measurements of this shape have been **multiplied by 3**, therefore, **scale factor 3** has been used.

Worked examples

1 What scale factor has been used to enlarge shape **A** to create shape **B**?

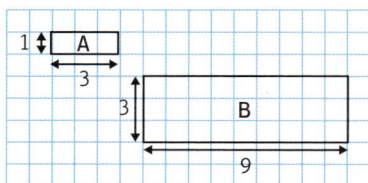

All the measurements in this rectangle have been **multiplied by 3** Therefore, **scale factor 3** has been used.

Scale factor 3

2 Jessica uses a scale factor of 2 to enlarge her triangle (1) on a coordinate grid. She has already drawn one side of the enlarged triangle. Where will point C of the enlarged triangle (2) be?

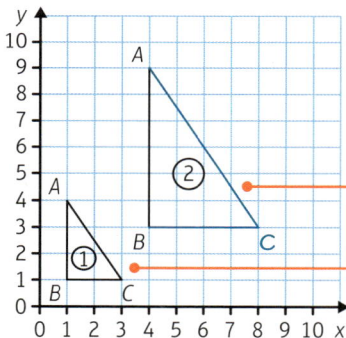

123 Remember, when using coordinates, read **along (x-axis)**, then **up (y-axis)** and write the grid reference with a comma and in brackets as shown.

$A = (4, 9)$, $B = (4, 3)$. Read **along** the x-axis then **up** the y-axis to find point C.

$A = (1, 4)$, $B = (1, 1)$, $C = (3, 1)$

Point C of triangle 2 is at _____ (8, 3) _____

3 Ben is drawing shapes. Circle the shape that is an enlargement of shape **Y** with scale factor 1.5

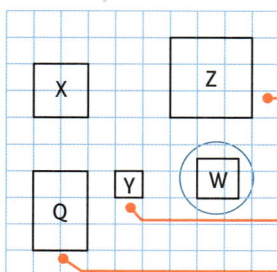

This shape is 3 cm by 3 cm. It has been enlarged from shape **Y** using a scale factor of 3

The original shape **Y** is 1 cm by 1 cm.

This shape is a rectangle, so it can't be the answer.

Guided questions

1 Identify the scale factor used to enlarge shape **A** to get shape **B**.

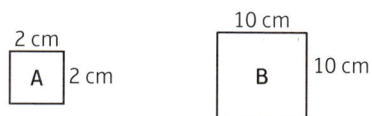

2 cm

A | 2 cm

10 cm

B | 10 cm

$10 \div 2 = 5$

_____

2 Enlarge shape **C** using a scale factor of 3

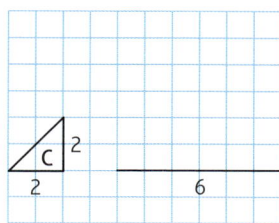

To enlarge a shape by a scale factor of 3, make all of the measurements 3 times larger. The base of the triangle will be 6 squares long (2×3)

C | 2
2 | 6

3 Shape **G** is going to be enlarged by a scale factor of 4

What will its new dimensions (measurements) be?

_b_ 6 cm

_a_ 2 cm

G

2 cm

_c_ 8 cm

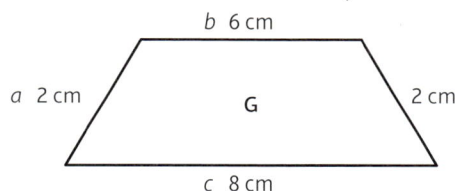

All four sides of this trapezium will be 4 times longer.

$a =$ _____ 8 _____ cm $b =$ _____ cm $c =$ _____ cm

4 Enlarge the shape **R** by a scale factor of 0.5

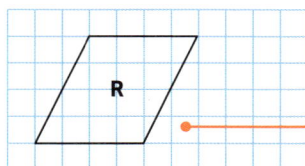

R

123 When enlarging by a number smaller than 1, the shape **reduces** in size. This is called **fractional enlargement**.

This shape is 4 squares $\times$ 4 squares.

When enlarging by 0.5, the shape will actually get smaller. $0.5 = \frac{1}{2}$, so all the measurements will be half their original size.

5 This shape has been enlarged by scale factor 5

What are the measurements of the original shape?

_A_ 20 cm

_B_ 5 cm

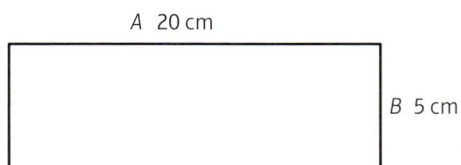

Side A has been enlarged to 20 cm by a scale factor of 5
To find its original length, divide by 5

$A =$ _____ 4 _____ cm $B =$ _____ cm

Have a go

1 What scale factor has been used to enlarge shape **A** to get shape **B**?

3 cm   3 cm   **A**   3 cm   3 cm

12 cm   12 cm   **B**   12 cm   12 cm

> Work out how much each measurement has increased by to find the scale factor.

1 mark

_____

2 The equilateral triangle **Z** is enlarged by a scale factor of 3
Circle the correct enlargement of the shape.

> Apply the scale factor to **all** the shape's measurements to find the answer.

> Use times tables facts to check the scale factors.

2   2   **Z**   2

6   **W**   6   4

6   **Y**   6   6

4   **T**   4   4

2   **X**   5   6

1 mark

3 The shape on the left is enlarged by a scale factor of 5 to get the shape on the right. What are the missing measurements?

> Multiply the original measurements by the scale factor.

10 cm   2 cm   2 cm   8 cm   8 cm   2 cm

a   b   c

$a =$ _____ cm

$b =$ _____ cm

$c =$ _____ cm

3 marks

4 Ben is building a model car. Its box is 15 cm long, 4 cm tall and 7 cm wide. The model will be longer than the box by a scale factor of 5. How many centimetres long will the model car actually be?

> Try sketching the box on a separate piece of paper to visualise this problem.

1 mark

_____ cm

Time to reflect

Mark your _Have a go_ section out of 6. How are you doing so far?

Check your answers in the back of the book and see how you are doing.

☐ **Had a go**	☐ **Nearly there**	☐ **Nailed it!**
0—2 marks	_3—5 marks_	_6 marks_
Have another look at the _Worked examples_ on page 54. Then try these questions again.	Look at your incorrect answers. Make sure you understand how to get the correct answer.	Congratulations! Now see whether you can get full marks on the _Timed practice_.

When you are ready, try the _Timed practice_ on the next page.

Timed practice

10

1 What scale factor has been used to enlarge parallelogram **W** to get parallelogram **X**?

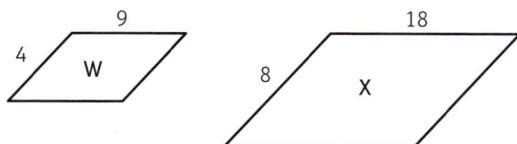

9
4
W

18
8
X

_____

1
mark

2 The shape on the left was enlarged by a scale factor of 1.5 to produce the shape on the right. Write the missing measurements.

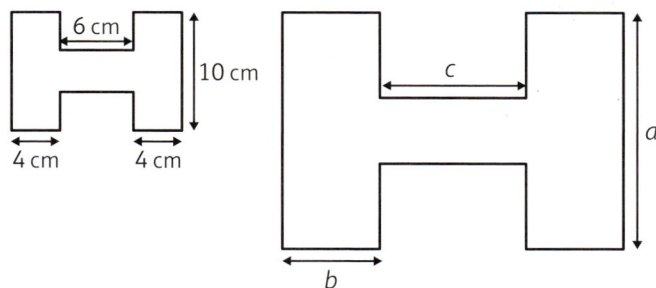

6 cm
10 cm
4 cm   4 cm

c
a
b

$a =$ _____ cm

$b =$ _____ cm

$c =$ _____ cm

3
marks

3 Tom is enlarging a rectangle on a coordinate grid using a scale factor of 4. Point *A* has been plotted. Where should Tom plot points *B*, *C* and *D*?

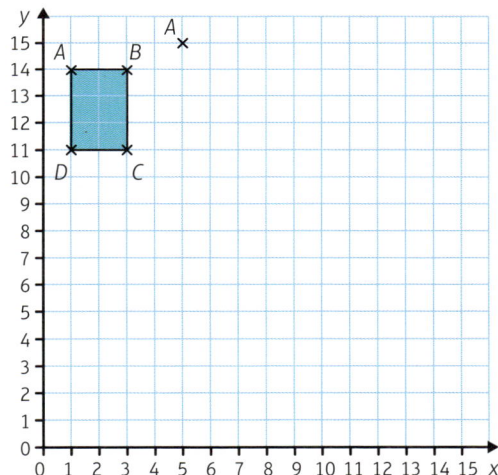

y
15 A   A ×
14 A × B ×
13
12
11 × ×
10 D   C
9
8
7
6
5
4
3
2
1
0
  0 1 2 3 4 5 6 7 8 9 10 11 12 13 14 15 x

$B =$ _____

$C =$ _____

$D =$ _____

3
marks

4 Class 4 are planning a mural. They draw a sketch of their mural, which is 50 cm tall and 42 cm wide. They plan to enlarge the sketch by a scale factor of 2.5 when creating the actual mural. Complete the sentence.

The mural will be _____ cm tall and _____ cm wide.

2
marks

Time to reflect

Mark your *Timed practice* section out of 9. How did you do?

Check your answers in the back of the book and write your score in the progress chart.

☐ *0–7 marks*
  Scan the QR code for extra practice.
Then, move on to the next practice section or
try Test 12 in the Ten-Minute Tests book.

☐ *8–9 marks*
  Well done!
Move on to the next practice section or try
Test 12 in the Ten-Minute Tests book.

Checkpoint 2

In this checkpoint you will practise skills from the **Fractions, decimals and percentages** topic, as well as the **Ratio and proportion** topic. There are 14 questions for you to answer.

15

1 Write $2\frac{3}{4}$ as an improper fraction.

Section 8

1 mark

_____

2 Write $\frac{11}{3}$ as a mixed number.

Section 8

1 mark

_____

3 Circle the pair of equivalent fractions.

Section 10

$\frac{3}{4}$ and $\frac{5}{8}$ $\frac{6}{18}$ and $\frac{1}{3}$ $\frac{5}{10}$ and $\frac{2}{3}$ $\frac{8}{15}$ and $\frac{8}{14}$

1 mark

4 Write each fraction in its simplest form.

Section 8

a $\frac{8}{16} =$ _____

b $\frac{4}{24} =$ _____

3 marks

c $\frac{3}{15} =$ _____

5 Complete the chart.

Section 10

Percentage	Decimal	Fraction
95%	**a** _____	$\frac{95}{100}$
b _____	0.33	$\frac{33}{100}$
56%	0.56	**c** _____

3 marks

6 What is 25% of 74?

Section 9

1 mark

_____

7 What is 60% of 130?

Section 9

1 mark

_____

8 A scarf is normally priced at £12. It is reduced by 15% in a sale. What is the new price of the scarf?

Section 9

1 mark

£ _____

9 Circle the value which is not equivalent in each group.

a
$\frac{72}{100}$
7.2%
0.72

b
$\frac{1}{5}$
$\frac{20}{100}$
25%

c
0.03
3%
$\frac{3}{10}$

Section 10

3 marks

10 Use <, > and = symbols to complete these statements correctly.

a 10% ☐ 0.01

b $\frac{2}{4}$ ☐ 0.5

c 95% ☐ 0.99

Section 10

3 marks

11 Shahina has 12 small stick insects and 36 large stick insects. What is the ratio of large to small stick insects? Give your answer in its simplest form.

_____

Section 11

1 mark

12 Chris and Maimuna share 52 playing cards out using a ratio of 1 : 3, with Chris having the smaller share.

How many playing cards does Maimuná get?

_____

Section 11

1 mark

13 What scale factor has been used to enlarge this shape?

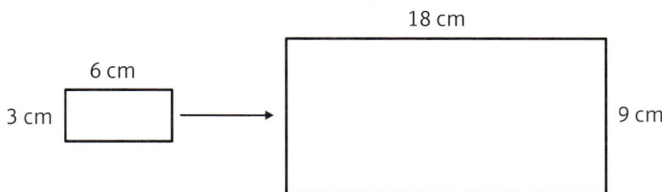

6 cm

3 cm

18 cm

9 cm

Section 12

1 mark

_____

14 Theo draws a square with sides of 5 cm. If he uses a scale factor of 6 to enlarge his square, what will the side lengths be?

_____ cm

Section 12

1 mark

Time to reflect

Mark your *Checkpoint* out of 22. How did you do?

1 Check your answers in the back of the book and write your score in the progress chart. If any of your answers are incorrect, use the section links to find out which practice sections to look at again.

2 Scan the QR code for extra practice.

3 Move on to the next practice section.

13 Converting units

In the 11+ test, you might be asked to convert between metric units such as grams and kilograms, or millimetres, centimetres, metres and kilometres. You might also be asked to convert between measurements of time and to know rough equivalence between imperial (old) and metric (modern) units.

Before you begin

Metric units

You can convert easily between metric units using multiplying and dividing by 10, 100 and 1000

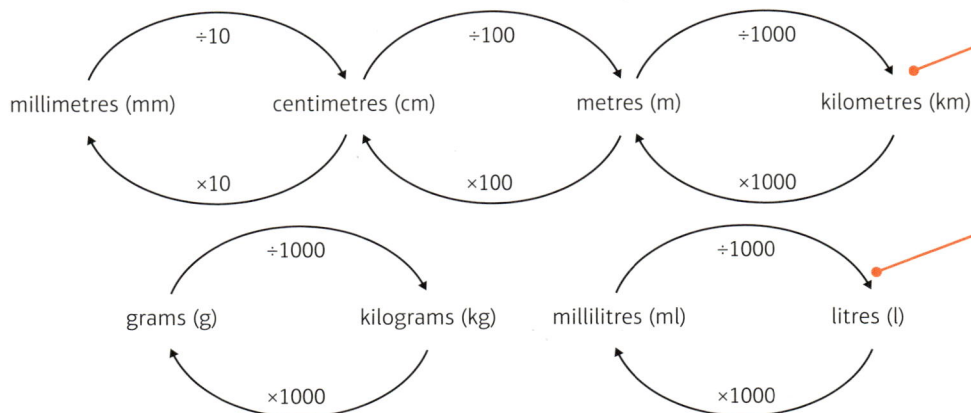

millimetres (mm) ÷10 centimetres (cm) ÷100 metres (m) ÷1000 kilometres (km)

×10   ×100   ×1000

grams (g) ÷1000 kilograms (kg)   millilitres (ml) ÷1000 litres (l)

×1000   ×1000

> Millimetres, centimetres, metres and kilometres are used to measure **length and distance**. 150 cm is equal to 1500 mm or 1.5 m.

> Millilitres and litres are used to measure **capacity** (the space a liquid takes up). 2.5 l is the same as 2500 ml.

> Grams and kilograms are used to measure **mass** (or weight). 1 kg = 1000 g.

Imperial units

Use these conversions to find approximate **equivalence** between metric and imperial units in problems.

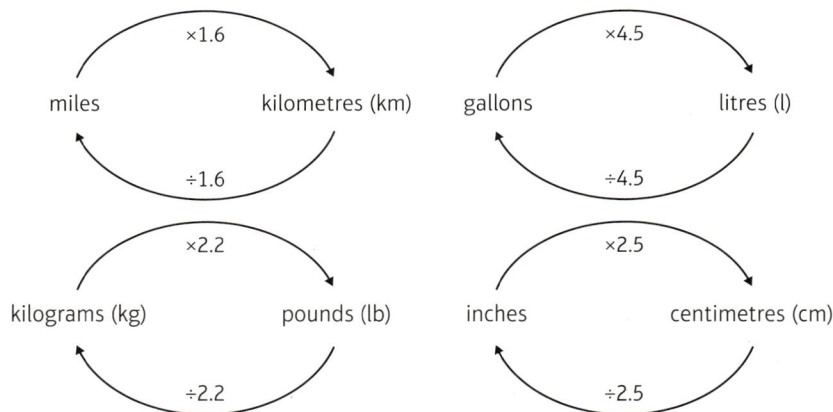

miles ×1.6 kilometres (km)   gallons ×4.5 litres (l)
×1.6 ÷1.6   ÷4.5

kilograms (kg) ×2.2 pounds (lb)   inches ×2.5 centimetres (cm)
÷2.2   ÷2.5

> Miles are used to measure **distance**.

> Gallons are used to measure **capacity** such as amounts of vehicle fuel.

> Pounds (lbs) are still sometimes used in cooking to measure **mass (weight)**. There are 16 ounces (oz) in 1 lb and 1 oz ≈ 25 g.

> **123** The symbol ≈ is used to show approximate equivalence.

> Feet and **inches** are an imperial measure of **length** and are often used for height. 12 inches = 1 foot (ft) ≈ 30 cm.

Time

Time is measured in seconds, minutes, hours, days, weeks, months and years.

> A leap year occurs once every 4 years. 2016 and 2020 are both leap years.

Worked examples

1 A watering can contains 2700 ml. Circle the correct amount in litres (l).

2 l   (2.7 l)   2.7 ml   27 000 l

> There are 1000 ml in 1 l, so we need to divide 2700 by 1000 to convert millilitres to litres. 2700 ÷ 1000 = 2.7

2 Ben travels 6 miles. Approximately how many kilometres is this? Circle the correct answer.

3 km   (9.6 km)   96 km   10 km

> To convert miles to kilometres, multiply by 1.6 You can get an approximate answer by multiplying by 1.5 mentally.
> 6 × 1.5 = 9, so the answer must be 9.6

Guided questions

1 A flask holds 2.5 litres of tea. How much tea is this in millilitres?

_____ millilitres

> There are 1000 ml in 1 litre.
> To convert litres into millilitres, multiply 2.5 by 1000

2 A 2 m ribbon is cut into 10 cm lengths. How many pieces of ribbon are made?

_____

> 1 m = 100 cm.

3 Joanna fills boxes with melons. Each fruit weighs roughly 250 g.
What will a box of five melons weigh? Circle the two correct answers.

125 g   1250 g   ~~1250 kg~~   1.25 kg   1.25 g

> 5 × 250 = 1250. There are 1250 g per box.

> The wrong unit has been used here.

4 Terry walks 16.4 km. How many metres is this?

_____ metres

> To convert 1250 g to kilograms, divide by 1000

> To convert kilometres to metres, multiply by 1000

5 A cereal factory packs boxes with 200 g of cornflakes. It can produce 50 boxes an hour. How many kilograms of cornflakes are packed in 1 hour?

_____ kilograms

> **1** Work out the amount in grams packed in 1 hour. 200 g × 50 = 10 000 g.
> **2** Convert grams to kilograms by dividing by 1000

6 Leela works as a train driver for 25 hours a month. How many hours does Leela work each year?

_____ hours

> There are 12 months every year, so you need to multiply Tina's monthly hours by 12

7 The distance from Northville to Southville is 16 miles. Circle the approximate distance in kilometres.

25.6 km   9.6 km   10.5 km   30.2 km

> To convert miles into km you must multiply by 1.6
> You can mentally multiply by 1.5 to get an approximate answer. 16 × 1.5 = 24

8 Steve took 1 hour 38 minutes to complete a swimathon. Harry took half this time. What was Harry's time?

_____ minutes

> There are 60 minutes in an hour, so 1 hour 38 minutes is the same as 98 minutes. To find Harry's time, divide this number by 2

Beyond the exam

Guess how many days or weeks there are in a million seconds. Now work out the answer and see how close you were. See if you can work out how many seconds there are in a year. Remember, there are 365 days in one year.

Have a go

1 A book measures 320 mm along its spine. What is its length in centimetres?

> There are 10 mm in every 1 cm.

_____ cm

`1 mark`

2 Dillon goes to the gym every day. He does 43 days in a row. How many whole weeks is this?

_____ weeks

> There are seven days in one week.

`1 mark`

3 Gerry has a 3 litre bottle of orange juice. His family drink half of the juice.

a How much is left in litres?

_____ litres

b Convert your answer to millilitres.

> 1 litre is equal to 1000 ml.

_____ millilitres

`2 marks`

4 Sarah jogs every day. Her daily run takes her on an 8.2 km circuit. Circle the number of metres she runs per day.

820 m   8200 m   82 000 m   0.0082 m

> 1 km is equal to 1000 m.

`1 mark`

5 A bag of salt and vinegar crisps weighs 25 g. How much does a multipack of 10 weigh? Give your answer both in grams and in kilograms.

_____ grams

_____ kilograms

> 25 g is equal to 0.025 kg.

`2 marks`

6 Jasper, a prize-winning python, measures 4200 mm. How long is Jasper in metres? Circle the correct answer.

4.2 cm   4.2 m   42 cm   42 mm

`1 mark`

7 Ben is baking a cake. The recipe calls for 6 oz of flour, but his scales only measure in grams and kilograms. Approximately how many grams of flour should Ben use?

_____ grams

`1 mark`

Time to reflect

Mark your _Have a go_ section out of 9. How are you doing so far?

Check your answers in the back of the book and see how you are doing.

Had a go	**Nearly there**	**Nailed it!**
0–4 marks	_5–8 marks_	_9 marks_
Have another look at the _Worked examples_ on page 60. Then try these questions again.	Look at your incorrect answers. Make sure you understand how to get the correct answer.	Congratulations! Now see whether you can get full marks on the _Timed practice_.

When you are ready, try the _Timed practice_ on the next page.

Timed practice

⏱ **10**

1 Complete the table to show conversion between millimetres, centimetres and metres.

Millimetres	Centimetres	Metres
a _____	200 cm	2 m
1 500 000 mm	**b** _____	1500 m
20 000 mm	2000 cm	**c** _____

3 marks

2 Becky has been working as a juggler in the circus for 48 months. How many years is this?

_____ years

1 mark

3 Jack has 3 cans of cola. Each can contains 300 ml. How much cola does Jack have altogether?

a _____ litres

b _____ millilitres

2 marks

4 Mr Johnston eats a 50 g apple every day for 3 weeks. Circle the weight of the total amount of apples he eats.

150 g   1550 g   1.5 kg   1050 g

1 mark

5 The benches in a nursery class are 300 mm tall. Convert this to centimetres and to metres.

_____ centimetres

_____ metres

2 marks

6 Neil has knitted a scarf that is 20 inches long. How long is this in centimetres?

_____ centimetres

1 mark

7 Polly drives 500 miles in one week. Circle the equivalent distance in kilometres.

804 km   84 km   840 km   8400 km

1 mark

Time to reflect

Mark your *Timed practice* section out of 11. How did you do?
Check your answers in the back of the book and write your score in the progress chart.

☐ *0–9 marks*
Scan the QR code for extra practice.
Then move on to the next practice section or
try Test 13 in the Ten-Minute Tests book.

☐ *10–11 marks*
Well done!
Move on to the next practice section or try
Test 13 in the Ten-Minute Tests book.

14 Perimeter

In the 11+ test you will need to be able to find the perimeter of various shapes, including squares, rectangles and other shapes made from squares and rectangles (composite shapes). You will also need to know how to find missing side lengths.

Before you begin

Perimeter

Perimeter is a measurement of the **distance** around the outside of a shape. **Addition** is used to calculate perimeter.

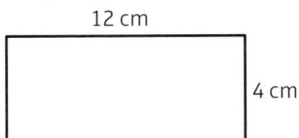

12 cm
4 cm

To find the perimeter of this rectangle, **add** together the lengths for **all four sides**. $12\,cm + 12\,cm + 4\,cm + 4\,cm = 32\,cm$.

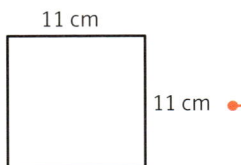

123 Remember that squares have **four** equal sides and rectangles have **two pairs** of equal sides.

11 cm
11 cm

To find the perimeter of the square, calculate $11\,cm + 11\,cm + 11\,cm + 11\,cm = 44\,cm$. For squares, you can also **multiply** the length of one side by 4

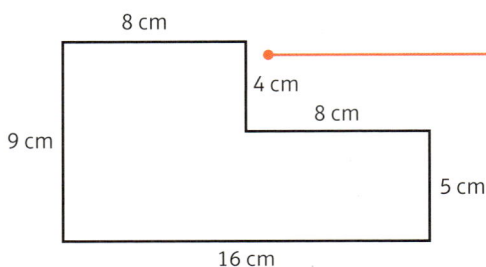

8 cm
4 cm
8 cm
9 cm
5 cm
16 cm

To find the perimeter of this shape, work out $9\,cm + 8\,cm + 4\,cm + 8\,cm + 5\,cm + 16\,cm = 50\,cm$.

This composite shape has more sides than a quadrilateral, so it is important to **check** you have added together **all** the lengths.

Worked example

1 Find the perimeter of this shape.

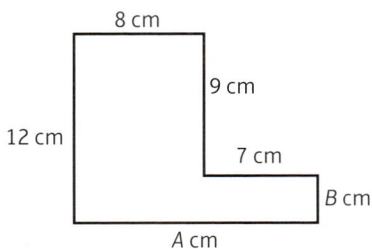

8 cm
9 cm
12 cm
7 cm
B cm
A cm

$A = 8 + 7 = 15\,cm$

$B = 12 - 9 = 3\,cm$

Perimeter $= 12 + 8 + 9 + 7 + 3 + 15 = 54\,cm$

_____54_____ cm

You need to find the length of side A. Look at the horizontal side lengths on the opposite side of the shape.

The vertical side on the left is 12 cm, so the two vertical sides on the right must add up to 12
$B + 9\,cm = 12$, so $B = 3\,cm$.

Guided questions

1 Find the perimeter of the square.

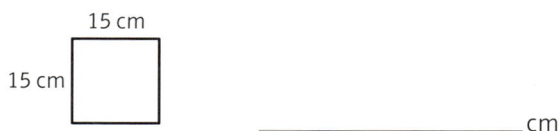

15 cm

15 cm

_____ cm

> You can use either addition or multiplication because all four sides measure 15 cm.

2 Find the perimeter of the rectangle.

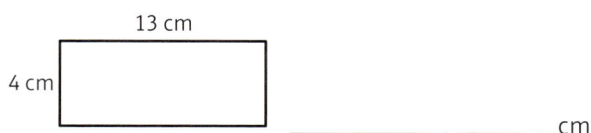

13 cm

4 cm

_____ cm

> Rectangles have two pairs of equal sides, so you need to add together two lots of 4 cm and two lots of 13 cm to find the perimeter.

3 Alex has some rectangular tiles that are 5 cm wide and 8 cm long. She uses three tiles to make a new shape. Find the perimeter of the shape.

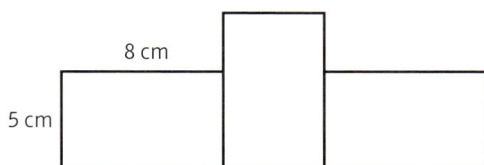

8 cm

5 cm

> Use the dimensions of the tile to work out the side lengths of the shape. To find the two shortest side lengths: 8 cm − 5 cm = 3 cm

_____ cm

4 Find the perimeter of this shape.

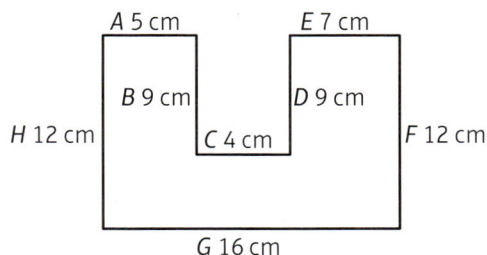

A 5 cm   E 7 cm

B 9 cm   D 9 cm

H 12 cm   C 4 cm   F 12 cm

G 16 cm

> **1** H and F are both 12 cm. 12 + 12 = 24
> **2** B and D are both 9 cm. 9 + 9 = 18
> **3** A + C + E = 16 cm. G is also 16 cm. 16 + 16 = 32
> **4** Add these 3 numbers together: 24 + 18 + 32

_____ cm

5 David draws a square which has a perimeter of 1.2 m. What is the measurement of each side in centimetres?

> Squares have 4 equal sides so divide the perimeter by 4 to find the length of each side.

> Remember to convert the perimeter from metres to centimetres.

_____ cm

Beyond the exam

Draw a shape like this on a piece of paper. Make sure the end of the line meets up with the start, and that your line does not cross itself.

Guess the perimeter of your shape, then use a piece of string and a ruler to check how accurate your guess was.

Have a go

3 marks

1 Three shapes have been drawn on a centimetre-square grid. Work out the perimeter of each shape.

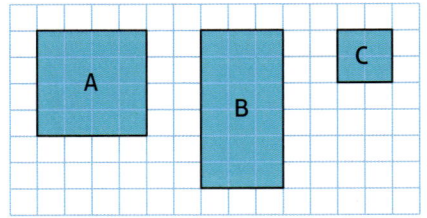

A _____ cm

B _____ cm

C _____ cm

1 mark

2 Farmer Paul has a square field which measures 50 m on each side. What is the perimeter of his field?

_____ m

1 mark

3 Georgina has made a rectangular cake. The longer sides each measure 22 cm and the shorter sides each measure 15 cm. What length of ribbon does Georgina need to fit around the outside of her cake?

_____ cm

> Rectangles have two pairs of equal sides.

1 mark

4 Circle the shape with the longest perimeter.

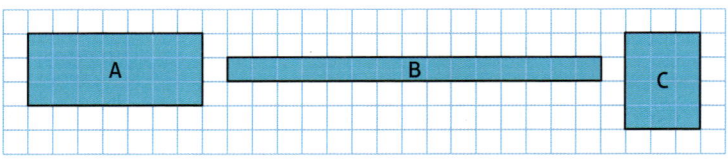

2 marks

5 Fencing comes in 10 m lengths. Sarah wants to fence her allotment which is a rectangle measuring 4 m by 7 m.

How many whole lengths of fencing will she need to buy and how much will be left over?

whole lengths: _____ left over: _____ m

> Find the perimeter of the allotment and divide it by 10

> Use the given lengths to identify those that are missing.

1 mark

6 Find the perimeter of this shape.

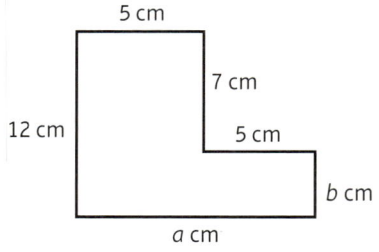

5 cm

7 cm

12 cm

5 cm

b cm

a cm

_____ cm

Time to reflect

Mark your *Have a go* section out of 9. How are you doing so far?

Check your answers in the back of the book and see how you are doing.

☐ **Had a go**
0–4 marks
Have another look at the *Worked examples* on page 64. Then try these questions again.

☐ **Nearly there**
5–8 marks
Look at your incorrect answers. Make sure you understand how to get the correct answer.

☐ **Nailed it!**
9 marks
Congratulations! Now see whether you can get full marks on the *Timed practice*.

When you are ready, try the *Timed practice* on the next page.

Timed practice

10

1 Find the perimeters of shapes **A**, **B** and **C**.

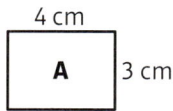
4 cm
A 3 cm

8.5 cm
B 2.5 cm

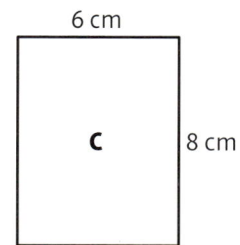
6 cm
C 8 cm

A _____ cm   B _____ cm   C _____ cm

3 marks

2 Gemma ran three laps of a square field. The field measures 12 m along each side. Circle the distance Gemma ran.

144 m   48 m   120 m   124 m

1 mark

3 Find the perimeter of this shape.

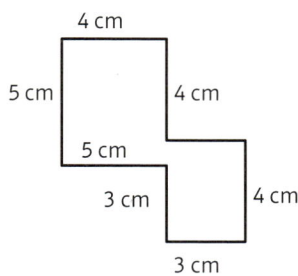
4 cm
5 cm
4 cm
5 cm
3 cm
4 cm
3 cm

_____ cm

1 mark

4 Three of these shapes have the same perimeter. Circle the odd one out.

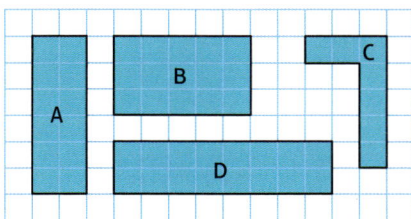
A
B
C
D

1 mark

5 Mrs Choudhury is putting a border around a classroom display. The display is a rectangle measuring 60 cm by 120 cm. Circle the length of border needed.

3.6 cm   3.6 m   36 cm   360 m

1 mark

6 A rectangular mat has a perimeter of 20 m. It is 7 m long. What is the width of the mat?

_____ m

1 mark

Time to reflect

Mark your *Timed practice* section out of 8. How did you do?

Check your answers in the back of the book and write your score in the progress chart.

☐ *0–6 marks*
Scan the QR code for extra practice.
Then, move on to the next practice section or try Test 14 in the Ten-Minute Tests book.

☐ *7–8 marks*
Well done!
Move on to the next practice section or try Test 14 in the Ten-Minute Tests book.

15 Area

In the 11+ test, you might be asked to find areas of rectangles. You will also need to be able to compare the areas of shapes and use a simple formulae.

Before you begin

Area

Area is a measurement of the **space covered by a shape**. You can use **multiplication** to calculate areas of rectangles.

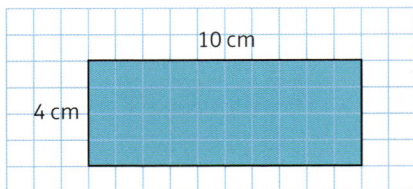

10 cm
4 cm

This rectangle **covers** 40 squares. It is 10 squares long and 4 squares wide. To find the area, multiply these numbers together.
$4 \times 10 = 40$ squares

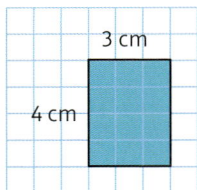

123   Use the formula **area = length × width**.

3 cm
4 cm

area = length × width: $4\,cm \times 3\,cm = 12\,cm^2$

When writing units of area, use the **squared** symbol (a small, raised 2) just after the units to show that you are measuring something **two dimensional**, rather than just a straight line.

These two rectangles both have an **area** of $12\,cm^2$. However, their **perimeters** are not the same. You will also find that shapes with the same perimeters can have **different** areas.

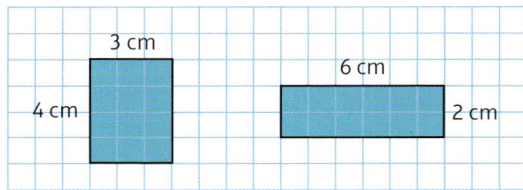

3 cm
4 cm

6 cm
2 cm

Area = $12\,cm^2$
Perimeter = 14 cm

Area = $12\,cm^2$
Perimeter = 16 cm

Worked example

1 Find the area of this shape.

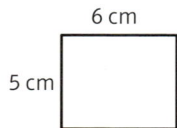

6 cm
5 cm

Length × width = area. The rectangle covers a space the size of 30 square centimetres.

$6\,cm \times 5\,cm = 30\,cm^2$

_____30_____ cm²

Beyond the exam

At secondary school, you might be asked to cover your exercise books with paper or sticky-backed plastic. Measure the outside covers of some exercise books. Add them together to calculate the area needed for several books. Don't forget to allow a little extra for folding inside to get a neat edge.

Guided questions

1 Find the area of this shape.

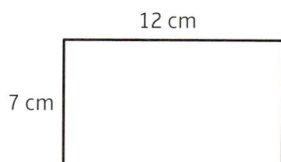

12 cm

7 cm

_____ cm²

> The length of this shape is 12 cm and the width is 7 cm, so you need to calculate 12 cm × 7 cm.

2 Tom's bedroom is 7 metres long and 5 metres wide. Circle its area.

12 cm²   35 cm²   35 m²   24 m²

> Multiply the length by the width. Think carefully about the units.

3 The measurements on these shapes are shown in cm. Tick the two shapes with the same area.

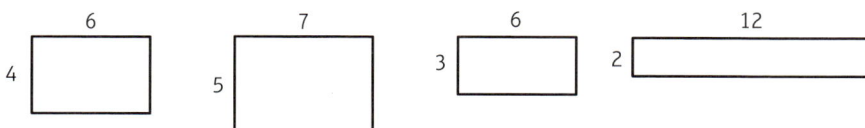

6

4

7

5

6

3

12

2

> Find the area of each shape and compare them.

4 Complete the chart of areas and perimeters of rectangles.

Length	Width	Area	Perimeter
8 cm	12 cm	a _____	40 cm
10 cm	8 cm	80 cm²	b _____
c _____	5 cm	45 cm²	28 cm

> Area = length × width

> The perimeter is the total of the lengths of all the sides.

> If you know the area of a shape, you need to do the inverse of multiplying to find missing side lengths. Calculate 45 ÷ 5

5 Henry owns a football stadium. He wants to find out the area of the pitch to work out the cost of covering it in artificial turf. The pitch is a rectangle. It is 90 m long and 50 m wide.

a What is the area of the pitch?

_____ m²

> **1** Area = length × width. You know the length is 90 m.
> **2** 90 × 50 will give the area. You can work out 9 × 50 = 450 then times by 10
> Give the answer in m².

b The turf comes in 2 m × 2 m squares. How many squares of turf does Henry need to buy to cover the pitch?

_____

> **1** Each square is 2 m × 2 m, so 4 m².
> **2** Divide the area of the pitch by the area of one square.

6 A rectangle has a length of 6.3 cm and a width of 5.8 cm. Estimate the area in cm² by rounding the side lengths to the nearest whole number.

_____ cm²

> 6.3 cm rounds to 6 cm.

> Once you have rounded, multiply the whole numbers to find the approximate area.

Have a go

3 marks

1 Find the areas of shapes **A**, **B** and **C**. Each square has an area of $1\,cm^2$.

A _____ cm^2

B _____ cm^2

C _____ cm^2

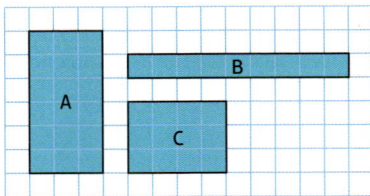

> Area = length $\times$ width

1 mark

2 A swimming pool has a diving section which is 9 m wide by 13 m long. What is its area?

_____ m^2

> Use the units m^2 or cm^2 to show that a two dimensional area is being measured.

1 mark

3 Jade is fitting a carpet in her bedroom. Her bedroom measures 3.5 m by 3 m. What area of carpet does she need to buy?

_____ m^2

> When multiplying decimals, the answer should have the total number of decimal places in all of the numbers in the question.

4 Circle the shape with the largest area.

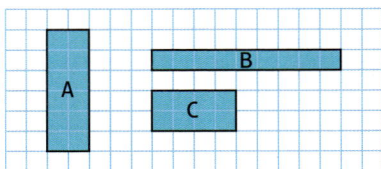

1 mark

5 A classroom has an area of $96\,m^2$. If the classroom is 12 m long, what is its width?

_____ m^2

> Use the inverse operation (division) to find the missing width.

1 mark

6 Circle the approximate area of this shape.

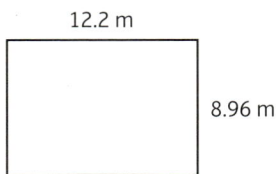

12.2 m

8.96 m

> Use rounding to estimate the answer.

$100\,m^2$ $117\,m^2$ $108\,m^2$ $96\,m^2$

Time to reflect

Mark your *Have a go* section out of 8. How are you doing so far?

Check your answers in the back of the book and see how you are doing.

☐ **Had a go**	☐ **Nearly there**	☐ **Nailed it!**
0–4 marks	*5–7 marks*	*8 marks*
Have another look at the *Worked example* on page 68. Then try these questions again.	Look at your incorrect answers. Make sure you understand how to get the correct answer.	Congratulations! Now see whether you can get full marks on the *Timed practice*.

When you are ready, try the *Timed practice* on the next page.

Timed practice

⏱ **10**

🔵 **1** Complete the table by filling in the missing lengths, widths and areas.

Length	Width	Area
10 mm	**a** _____	20 mm²
b _____	6 m	30 m²
12 cm	8 cm	**c** _____

3 marks

🔵 **2** Find the areas of these rectangles.

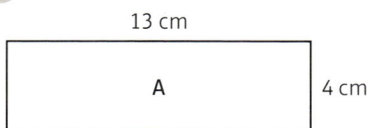

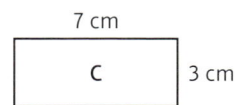

13 cm

| A | 4 cm |

21 cm

| B | 2 cm |

7 cm

| C | 3 cm |

a _____ cm²

b _____ cm²

c _____ cm²

3 marks

🟠 **3** Identify the shapes with:

a The same area

_____

b The same perimeter.

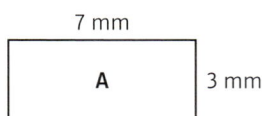

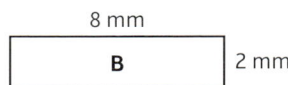

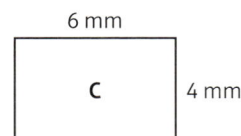

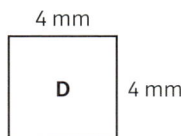

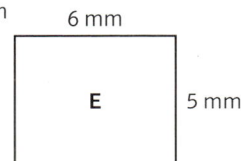

_____

7 mm

| A | 3 mm |

6 mm

| C | 4 mm |

8 mm

| B | 2 mm |

4 mm

| D | 4 mm |

6 mm

| E | 5 mm |

2 marks

🔵 **4** Chelsey has a yoga mat with an area of 3 m² and a width of 1.5 m. Circle the length of the mat.

2 cm   3.5 m   3 m   2 m

1 mark

🔵 **5** A school playground is 56.8 m long by 20.2 m wide. What is its approximate area? Round the measurements to the nearest 10 m.

_____ m²

1 mark

🔵 **6** The area of a rectangle is 60 cm. Circle the **two** possible combinations of length and width.

6 m × 10 m   6 cm × 0.10 m   3 cm × 20 cm   4 cm × 5 cm

1 mark

Time to reflect

Mark your *Timed practice* section out of 11. How did you do?
Check your answers in the back of the book and write your score in the progress chart.

☐ *0–9 marks*
   Scan the QR code for extra practice.
Then, move on to the next practice section or
try Test 15 in the Ten-Minute Tests book.

☐ *10–11 marks*
   Well done!
Move on to the next practice section or try
Test 15 in the Ten-Minute Tests book.

16 Reflections and translations

In the 11+ test, you may be asked to draw shapes using a four-quadrant coordinate grid. You will also need to be able to reflect and translate (move) shapes.

Before you begin

Reflections

When a shape is reflected, you see a **mirror image**. All its measurements and angles remain the same, but the shape appears to be flipped over.

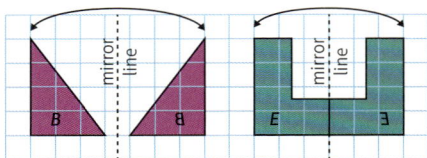

> These shapes have been **reflected**. The **mirror line** is shown by a dashed or dotted line. Sometimes the shape touches the mirror line and sometimes it doesn't.

> **123**   **Congruent** means that objects are the same shape and size. Both translations and reflections produce congruent shapes.

Translations

When a shape is **translated**, it is moved **horizontally** (sideways) or **vertically** (up or down), or sometimes **both**. All its measurements stay the same.

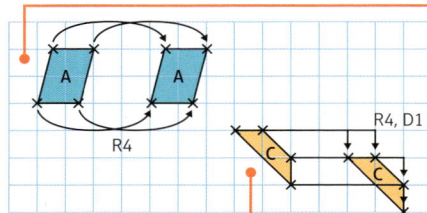

> This parallelogram has been translated 4 squares right (R4).

> Use the corners of shapes to count how by many squares the shapes have been translated.

> This trapezium has been translated 4 squares right and 1 square down (R4 and D1).

Coordinates

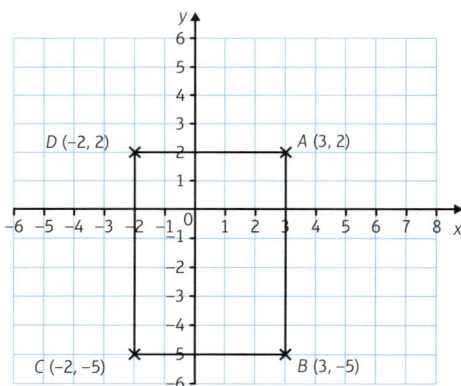

> The coordinate grid is split into four **quadrants**. **Negative numbers** are found on the left of the *x*-axis and the bottom of the *y*-axis.

> **123**   When you read or plot coordinates, always read the **x-axis** (horizontal axis) first, then the **y-axis** (vertical axis). **Coordinates** are written in brackets with a comma between them. Point *B* is at (3, −5), which means 3 along the *x*-axis and 5 down the *y*-axis.

Worked example

1   Write **reflection** or **translation** for each pair of shapes.

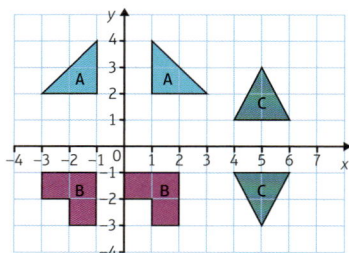

A   _____reflection_____

B   _____translation_____

C   _____reflection_____

> **A** has been reflected in the *y*-axis. **C** has been reflected in the *x*-axis. They both look like they are reflected in a mirror.

> **B** has been translated right by 3 squares. It has been shifted across, but the shape remains the same.

Guided questions

1 Reflect the triangle in the *y*-axis.

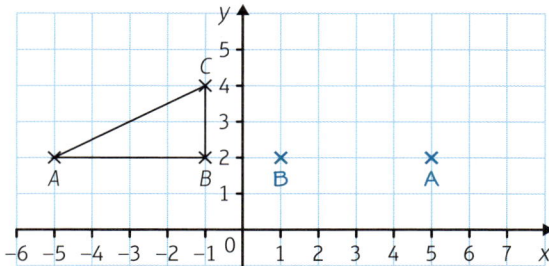

Reflecting a shape in the *y*-axis means you use the *y*-axis (vertical axis) as the mirror line.

2 Translate this rectangle down 3 and right 6

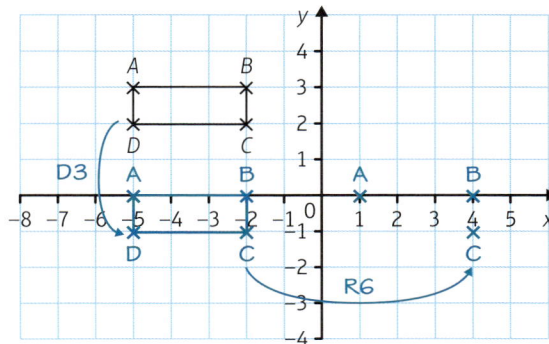

The shape must stay congruent (the same size).

3 Write the coordinates of points *A*, *B*, *C* and *D*.

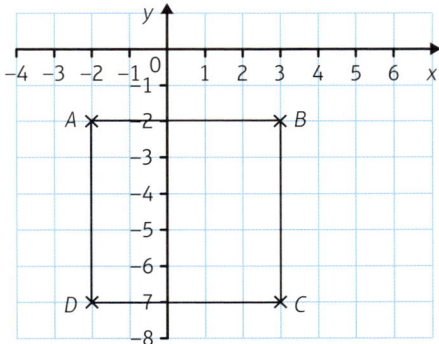

Read along the *x*-axis first, then up or down the *y*-axis.

A (−2, −2)   *B* (3, −2)   *C* (3, −7)   *D* (_____)

4 Tick true or false for the following statements.

	True	False
A has been translated down 3	☐	☐
B has been reflected in the *x*-axis.	☐	☐
C has been translated left 2	☐	☐

The shape has been reflected in the *y*-axis (horizontal axis).

Look at the shape and how it has moved.

The original shape and its translation are congruent. The original shape has moved down 3 squares on the grid.

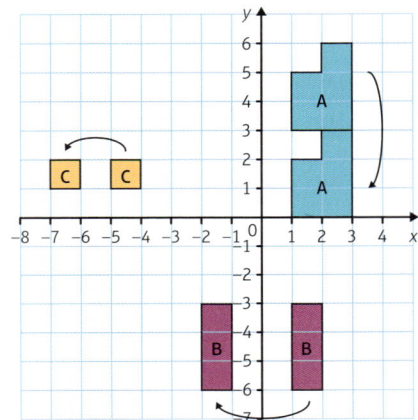

Have a go

1 Reflect this shape in the *y*-axis.

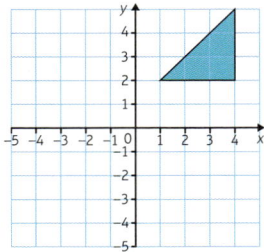

> The *y*-axis is the vertical axis. Remember that the shape should look like it has been flipped.

1 mark

2 Tick true or false for each statement.

	True	False
Reflections make a shape appear smaller.	☐	☐
Translated shapes remain the same size.	☐	☐
The *x*-axis runs vertically on the grid.	☐	☐

> Reflected and translated shapes remain congruent.

3 marks

3 Translate the shape right 6 and down 2

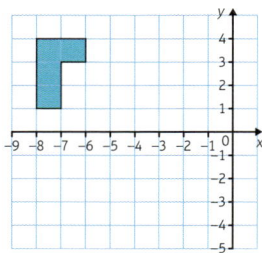

> Make sure your shape is the same size as the original shape.

1 mark

4 Look at the shapes in the diagram.

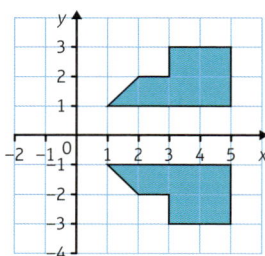

a Has the top shape been reflected or translated to get the bottom shape?

_____

b Describe the reflection or translation.

_____

> R = right, L = left, U = up and D = down.

2 marks

Time to reflect

Mark your *Have a go* section out of 7. How are you doing so far?

Check your answers in the back of the book and see how you are doing.

☐ **Had a go**	☐ **Nearly there**	☐ **Nailed it!**
0–2 marks	*3–6 marks*	*7 marks*
Have another look at the *Worked example* on page 72. Then try these questions again.	Look at your incorrect answers. Make sure you understand how to get the correct answer.	Congratulations! Now see whether you can get full marks on the *Timed practice*.

When you are ready, try the *Timed practice* on the next page.

Timed practice

10

1 Translate this shape left 4

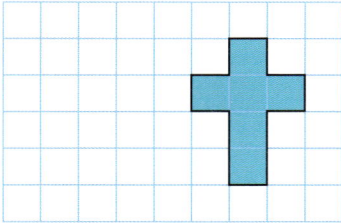

1 mark

2 Write the coordinates of the corners of this quadrilateral.

A _____   B _____

C _____   D _____

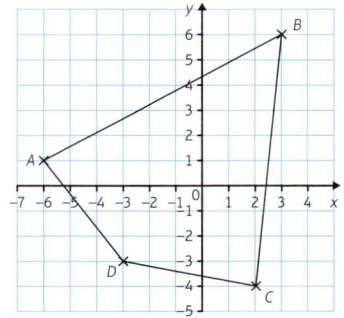

4 marks

3 If the trapezium is reflected in the *y*-axis, what will its new coordinates be?

A _____   B _____

C _____   D _____

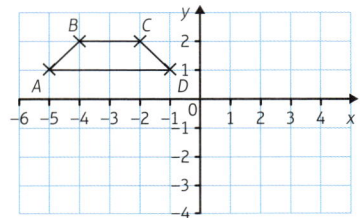

4 marks

4 Put ticks in the correct column to show whether each pair of shapes are reflections or translations.

	Reflection	Translation
A	☐	☐
B	☐	☐
C	☐	☐

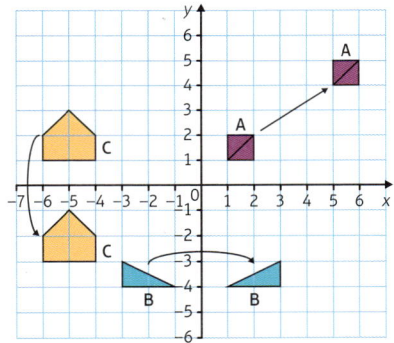

3 marks

5 Circle the pair of shapes that are congruent.

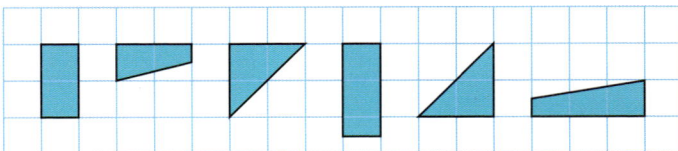

1 mark

Time to reflect

Mark your *Timed practice* section out of 13. How did you do?
Check your answers in the back of the book and write your score in the progress chart.

☐ *0–11 marks*
Scan the QR code for extra practice.
Then, move on to the next practice section or try Test 16 in the Ten-Minute Tests book.

☐ *12–13 marks*
Well done!
Move on to the next practice section or try Test 16 in the Ten-Minute Tests book.

Checkpoint 3

In this checkpoint you will practise skills from the **Shape and measurement** topic. There are 14 questions for you to answer.

(15)

1 mark

1 A barrel contains 73 litres of water. How many millilitres is this? Circle the correct measurement.

73 000 ml   7300 ml   730 000 ml   0.073 ml

Section 13

1 mark

2 A ball of wool is made of a string that is 2000 cm long. How long is this in metres?

_____ m

Section 13

1 mark

3 A pencil case measures 25 cm. Approximately how many inches is this?

_____ inches

Section 13

1 mark

4 Thierry drives for 30 miles. Approximately how many kilometres is this? Circle the most accurate distance.

30 km   15 km   45 km   300 km

Section 13

1 mark

5 Mr Green opens his shop every day for eight weeks without taking a day off. For how many days in a row does he work?

_____

Section 13

1 mark

6 Grace takes a train ride which lasts 75 minutes. Circle the equivalent time in hours.

7.50 hours   1.25 hours   0.75 hours   1.15 hours

Section 13

1 mark

7 A square field has sides of 15 m. What is its perimeter?

_____ m

Section 14

1 mark

8 Find the perimeter of this shape.

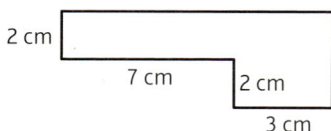

2 cm

7 cm

2 cm

3 cm

_____ cm

1 mark

9 Sam can buy wire netting in 20 m lengths. He has a square chicken enclosure with sides that are 24 m long. How many lengths of fencing will he need to surround the enclosure?

_____

Section 14

1 mark

10 A rectangular vegetable patch is 8 m long by 80 cm wide. What is its area?

_____ m²

Section 15

11 Which shape has the:

a greatest area: _____

b smallest area: _____

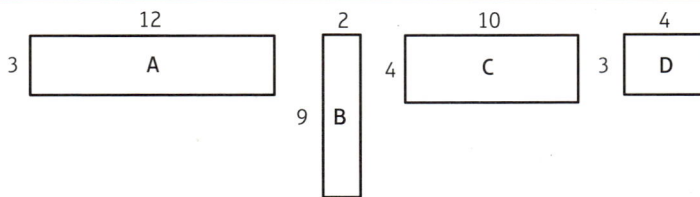

Section 15

2 marks

12 Tick to show whether these statements are true or false.

Section 16

	True	False
Reflected shapes get larger.	☐	☐
Translated shapes remain congruent.	☐	☐
The *y*-axis runs horizontally.	☐	☐

3 marks

13 Circle the correct translation for the shape.

Section 16

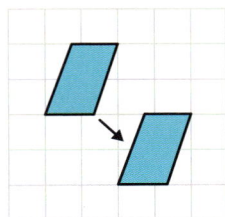

L3, U2   L2, D3   R2, D2   R2, D3

1 mark

14 Plot the following coordinates on the grid and draw the outline of the shape they make:
(−4, 2) (4, 2) (−3, 5) (3, 5)

Section 16

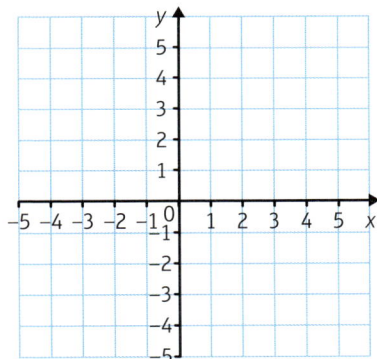

4 marks

Time to reflect

Mark your *Checkpoint out* of 20. How did you do?

1 Check your answers in the back of the book and write your score in the progress chart. If any of your answers are incorrect, use the section links to find out which practice sections to look at again.

2 Scan the QR code for extra practice.

Progress test

Complete this test once you have worked through all the practice sections in this book. It covers all the topics in this book and is as hard as a real 11+ test.

1 Write these numbers in order from highest to lowest.

| 89 897 | 89 798 | 894 798 | 8948 |

⬅ Section 1

1 mark

_____ _____ _____ _____

2 Round

⬅ Section 1

3 marks

a 8238 to the nearest 1000 _____

b 587 115 to the nearest 10 _____

c 9998 to the nearest 100 _____

3 In Moscow, the temperature is −12 °C. In Rome, the temperature is 30 °C. How much warmer is it in Rome than Moscow?

⬅ Section 2

1 mark

_____ °C

4 Write these numbers in order from lowest to highest.

| −15 | 12 | −8 | −5 |

⬅ Section 2

1 mark

_____ _____ _____ _____

5 Circle the false statement.

1 mark

a 5.63 to the nearest whole number = 6   **b** 3.019 to the nearest hundredth = 3.02

c 0.214 to the nearest tenth = 0.2   **d** 5.689 to the nearest tenth = 5.6

6 Complete the statements using the table.

⬅ Section 3

Runner	Race time in hours and minutes
Bert	4.58
Megan	3.49
Jamal	2.58
James	5.35

2 marks

a The runner with the slowest race time is _____ .

b The runner with the third quickest race time is _____ .

7 Write these modern numbers in Roman numerals.

Section 4

a 56 = _____

b 110 = _____

2 marks

8 Complete the calculation.

Section 4

_____ + 405 = 995

1 mark

9 Sam has one bank account containing £5300 and another containing £9152

Section 5

How much money does he have in total across the two accounts?

£ _____

1 mark

10 There are 15 533 seats in a football stadium and 12 300 are filled. How many seats are empty?

Section 5

_____

1 mark

11 Complete the table.

Section 6

Number	× 10	× 100	× 1000
365	3650	**a** _____	365 000
15.63	**b** _____	1563	**c** _____

3 marks

12 The entry fee for a trampoline park is £14.50

Section 6

How much would admission cost for 3 people?

£ _____

1 mark

13 Calculate 630 ÷ 70

Section 6

_____

1 mark

14 Calculate 52×63

Section 7

1 mark

_____

15 138 students go on a trip with 12 teachers. A coach holds 35 passengers. How many coaches should the school book for the trip?

Section 7

1 mark

_____

16 Write $\dfrac{26}{5}$ as a mixed number.

Section 8

1 mark

_____

17 Circle the fraction equivalent to $\dfrac{2}{3}$

Section 8

1 mark

$\dfrac{1}{3}$ $\dfrac{5}{6}$ $\dfrac{6}{9}$ $\dfrac{19}{20}$

18 Simplify each fraction.

Section 8

a $\dfrac{4}{16} =$ _____

b $\dfrac{4}{80} =$ _____

3 marks

c $\dfrac{15}{25} =$ _____

19 Complete the statements.

Section 9

a 99% as a fraction is _____ .

b 0.10 as a percentage is _____ %

3 marks

c If 55 squares on a hundred square are shaded, the percentage of unshaded squares is _____ %

20 Sally has 20 fish and 5 are stripy. What percentage of her fish are not stripy?

Section 9

1 mark

_____ %

21 Zaheer has a collection of green, red and yellow coloured marbles. 20% of them are green, $\dfrac{3}{5}$ are red. The rest are yellow. What percentage of his marbles are yellow?

Section 10

1 mark

_____ %

22 Write these values in order, starting with the highest.

Section 10

15%   1.5   0.22 $\dfrac{1}{5}$

1 mark

_____   _____   _____   _____

23 There are kittens for sale in a pet shop. Six are black and nine are tabby. What is the ratio of tabby kittens to black kittens? Give your ratio in its simplest form.

Section 11

1 mark

_____

24 Divide 32 into the following ratios.

Section 11

a 1:3

_____

b 3:5

2 marks

_____

25 What scale factor has been used to enlarge this isosceles triangle?

Section 12

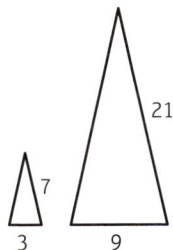

1 mark

_____

26 A rectangle has a length of 12 cm and an area of 84 cm². It is enlarged using a scale factor of 2.5

Section 12

What are the new dimensions of the rectangle?

length = _____ cm   width = _____ cm

2 marks

27 Convert 25.5 litres to millilitres.

Section 13

1 mark

_____ millilitres

28 Helen runs a 5.5 km race. How many metres is this?

Section 13

1 mark

_____ m

29 A cake recipe calls for 175 g of sugar. Approximately, how many ounces is this?

Section 13

1 mark

_____ oz $1\,oz = 25\,g$

30 Raj watches TV for 35 minutes each night for three nights. Circle the equivalent time in hours and minutes.

Section 13

1 mark

105 hours   1 hour 45 minutes   0.45 hours   1 hour 5 minutes

31 Find the perimeter of this shape in centimetres.

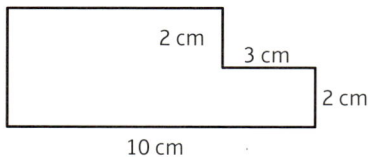

Section 14

2 cm

3 cm

2 cm

10 cm

1 mark

_____ cm

32 Samuel the guinea pig has a rectangular run in his owner's garden. The run has a length of 123 cm and width of 45 cm. What is the run's total perimeter in metres?

Section 14

1 mark

_____ m

33 A rectangular dining room is 13 m long by 7 m wide. What is its area?

Section 14

1 mark

_____ m^2

34 Describe the following translations.

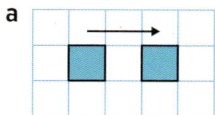

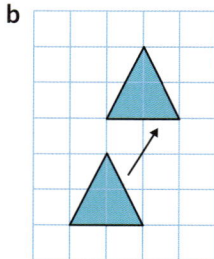

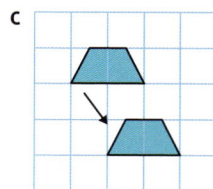

Section 16

a

b

c

3 marks

_____   _____   _____

35 What are the coordinates of the corners of the shape on the grid?

Section 16

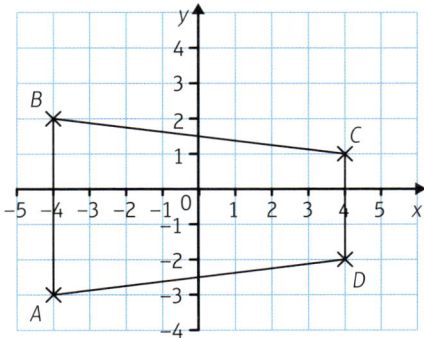

A _____

B _____

C _____

D _____

4 marks

36 Reflect this shape in the *x*-axis.

Section 16

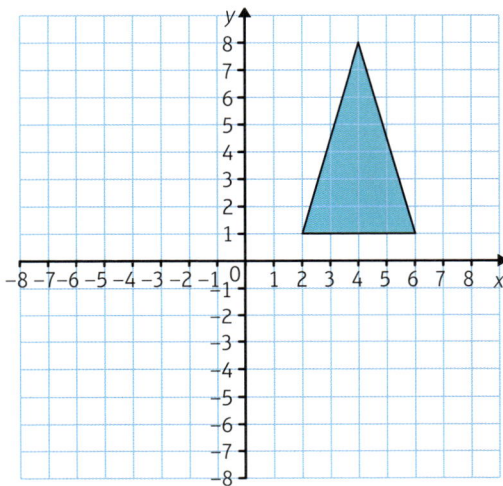

1 mark

Time to reflect

Mark your *Progress test* out of 53. How did you do?

☐ *0–44 marks*
Use the section links to identify your strengths and weaknesses. Revisit the practice sections you scored the lowest in and then scan the QR code to try more mixed questions.

☐ *45–53 marks*
Use the section links to identify your strengths and weaknesses. You might want to revisit the practice sections you scored the lowest in, before moving on to Practice Book 2.

Answers

Diagnostic test

Pages 2–7

1 6309, 63 023, 64 978, 697 001 ●━━━━━━━━━ 6309 only has 4 digits, all the others have 5 or 6

2 a 5680　　**b** 67 000　　**c** 723 500 ●━━━ When rounding, look one digit to the right. If it is 5 or more, round up. If it is 4 or less, round down.

3 15 ●━━━━━━━━━━━━━━ Counting up from −5 to zero is 5, and then from zero to 10 is 10

4 a −10　　**b** 8　　**c** −8 ●━━━━━━ Negative numbers with a larger digit have a lower value.

5 0.26 and 0.28 ●━━━━━━━ The sequence is in jumps of 0.02

6 a 10　　**b** 3.01　　**c** 9.3

7 a 7　　**b** 210

8 a 93　　**b** 1500 ●━━━━━━━ **a** XC = 90 and III = 3　　**b** M = 1000 and D = 500

9 £13 990

10 3212 ●━━━━━━━━━━━━ 5086 minus the number filled spaces gives 3212 spaces empty.

11 a 5.62　　**b** 489.7　　**c** 4.897 ●━━ Dividing by 10 means all digits move one place to the right. Dividing by 100, 2 places, dividing by 1000, 3 places.

12 £11.96

13 2000 ●━━━━━━━━━━━━ 5 × 4 = 20 so 50 × 40 = 2000

14 40 r2

15 27 ●━━━━━━━━━━━━━ Divide 324 by 12

16 $\frac{6}{5}$ ●━━━━━━━━━━━ In one whole there are 5 fifths, so there are six fifths in total.

17 a $\frac{1}{8}$　　**b** $\frac{1}{10}$　　**c** $\frac{1}{5}$ ●━━ Divide by highest common factors.

18 a 0.02　　**b** 99%　　**c** $\frac{11}{10}$

20% of the chickens don't lay eggs. 10% of 500 is 50. You can double this value to find 20%.

19 100 ●

$\frac{3}{10}$ is equal to 30%. Add the percentages together and subtract them from 100

20 60% ●

21 20% and 0.2 ●━━━━━ 2% is $\frac{2}{100}$ and $\frac{4}{5}$ is $\frac{8}{10}$

22 1:3 ●━━━━━━━━━━ 25 pine : 75 oak can be simplified using the highest common factor 25

23 a 50:100　　**b** 90:60 ●

a 150 ÷ 3 = 50
b 150 ÷ 5 = 30

24 5 ●

Both measurements have been multiplied by 5

25 length = 300 m　　width = 45 m ●

200 × 1.5 = 300 and 30 × 1.5 = 45

26 1.9 litres ●

The are 1000 ml in 1 litre, so convert 1900 ml to millilitres by dividing it by 1000

27 27.5 cm ●

1 inch is roughly the same as 2.5 cm. 2.5 × 11 = 27.5

28 4.5 km •————————— 1 mile is roughly the same as 1.6 km, so multiply the number of miles by 1.5 to get an approximate answer.

29 45 minutes •

30 48 m •

Quarter of an hour is 15 minutes.

$3 \times 15 = 45$ minutes, which is $\frac{3}{4}$ of an hour.

31 54 m •————————— Find the perimeter by adding together the lengths of all four sides.

32 702 m²

The missing lengths can be worked out using the lengths on the opposite side of the shape.

33 A, C, B, D •————————— A is 2 cm², **B** is 81 cm², **C** is 9 cm² and **D** is 16 m², so **D** is the largest.

34 R1, D4 •————————— The shape has moved right 1 square and down 4 squares.

35

Read along the x-axis first, then up or down the y-axis.

36 y •————————— The mirror line is vertical, so the shape has been reflected in the y-axis.

1 Ordering and rounding numbers

Page 9
Guided questions

1 **A** False   **B** True   **C** False

2 55 000 •

The number has 3 hundreds, so round it down, keeping the thousands digit the same.

3 45 465 •————————— This number has only 4 hundreds.

4 **a** 53 500   **b** 53 000 •

a There are 6 tens, so the hundreds round up.
b There are 4 hundreds, so the thousands digit remains the same.

Page 10
Have a go

1 320 000, 56 899, 56 898, 32 000, 5889, 320 •————————— Numbers with fewer digits are worth less, so appear last in the list.

2 **a** Bluefields Utd   **b** Kentville Utd •————————— 163 496 is the number with the greatest value, followed by 154 897

3 **a** 43 900   **b** 44 000   **c** 40 000

4 Rounded to the nearest thousand •————————— 639 000 has 3 zeros and 7 hundreds, so round up to the next thousand.

Page 11
Timed practice

There are 6 tens, so this number rounds up to the next ten.
There is a 1 in the thousand column, so this number rounds down to the nearest 10 000
There are nine hundreds, so round up to 1000

1 **a** 8590   **b** 850 000   **c** 1000   **d** 600 000 •

2 **a** 3567 is 4000 to the nearest thousand.
   b 39 647 is 39 600 to the nearest hundred.
   c 371 596 is 370 000 to the nearest ten thousand.
   d 56 897 is 60 000 to the nearest ten thousand.

There are fifty ten thousands, so round the hundreds of thousands up.

3 No •————————— 96 does round to 100, but Steve still only has 96 pence.

4 26 344, 260 231, 456 357, 456 375, 751 259, 824 675

5 **a** Magic Dust   **b** Star Kittens   **c** Cosmic Duo

2 Negative numbers

Guided questions

1 −10, −8, −6, −4, −2, 0, 2, 4, 6, 8, 10 •————— The sequence increases in jumps of 2

2 A 3 °C   B −3 °C   C −7 °C •————— The numbers get lower as you go further down the thermometer.

3 3 °C

4 31 °C •————— From 16, you can count back 16 °C to zero, then 15 °C down to minus 15. 16 + 15 = 31

5 a True   b False   c False

Page 14

Have a go

−3 is the nearest number to zero, so it is higher than the other numbers.

1 a 9   b 12   c −3 •

2 a −6   b −20   c −1 and −3 •————— **a** Count in 2s towards zero.   **b** Count down in 5s.
c Count in 1s.

3 −2 •

4 −17, −10, −3, 0 ————— Count back towards 0 from −7

5 14 °C

Page 15

Timed practice

1 Warmest temperature: 5 °C; Coldest temperature: −8 °C

2 −8, −2, 4 •————— This number line counts on in jumps of 2

3 a −1 < 7   b −6 > −10   c −8 < −4   d −12 > −21 •————— Negative numbers with a higher digit are less than those with lower digits.

4 −3

5 a −6   b 4   c −2   d −11 •————— When you add positive numbers to negative numbers, you move towards zero.

6 a +5   b 1   c 5

7 −4 °C •————— The temperature will be −6 °C in January and −5 °C in February, so in March it will be −4 °C.

3 Decimal numbers

Page 17

Guided questions

Although 0.1 has the fewest digits, it has the most tenths and therefore the highest value.

1 0.1 •

2 A 10.09 and 10.15 •————— The sequence counts up in jumps of 2 hundredths.

3 a Tomas   b Steve   c Nasreen •————— Write the times out in order: 11.02, 11.20, 11.56, 11.59

4 a 125.27   b 63.3   c 63.26
  d 5.6   e 3   f 3.00 •————— If the last digit of the number is 5 or more, round up. If it is 4 or less, round down.

5 65 litres ————— There are only 2 tenths in the number so the one digit remains the same.

Page 18

Have a go

1 2.095 •————— All the numbers have two whole ones. The answer has the fewest tenths.

2 Alba, Aziz and Ben •————— Use place value to compare the race times.

3 a 1.2   **b** 3.26   **c** 1   **d** 1.3

4 a £4.60   **b** £2.00   **c** £8.70

5 $6.3 > 0.6 \times 10$ •———————————— 0.6×10 is 6, which is worth less than 6.3

6 B 64.99 rounded to the nearest tenth •———— 64.99 rounds up to 65.0 and 65.22 rounds down to 65
   D 65.22 rounded to the nearest whole number

Page 19
Timed practice

1 5.256, 5.622, 56.25, 562.2

2 2.002, 0.222, 0.020, 0.002

3 a 4.6   **b** 4.56   **c** 5

4 a tenth   **b** hundredth   **c** whole number   **d** tenth

5 3.57 and 3.61

6 Alice is the most accurate. •———— Alice has rounded to the nearest pound, so has made the most accurate estimate. Jenny has rounded all the numbers up to the next multiple of 10 and Barney has rounded all the numbers to the nearest five pounds, so their estimates are less accurate.

4 Mental addition and subtraction

Page 21
Guided questions

1 $80\,000 + 60\,000 = 140\,000$ •———— Once you have partitioned the calculation, add your totals together to get the final answer.
   $9000 + 8000 = 17\,000$
   $500 + 500 = 1000$
   $60 + 20 = 80$
   $4 + 1 = 5$
   Final answer $= 158\,085$

2 £890 •———————————— Count back £50 to £900 and then another £10 to £890

3 898 •———————————— You can use the fact that 450 doubled is 900 to help you.

4 450 •———————————— $652 - 200 = 452$. Subtract 2 more to reach 450

5 1809 •———————————— M = 1000, DCCC = 800 and IX = 9

6 a MLXVI   **b** MCMXXVI   **c** MCMLXIX •———— M = 1000, CM = 900, LX = 60 and IX = 9

Page 22
Have a go

12 doubled is 24. The difference between 500 and 600 is 100, so 112 has been added.

1 a 112   **b** 248   **c** 1266

2 a 11281   **b** 35845   We only need to change the thousands and tens of thousands columns. The hundreds, tens and ones can stay the same.
   c 85463   **d** 270404 •———— 900 minus 500 becomes 400, so the hundreds digit changes. Only the tens and ones change. $96 - 92 = 4$

3 a 7   **b** 96   **c** 409 •————

VII is $5 + 2 = 7$
XC is $100 - 10 = 90$ and VI is $5 + 1 = 6$
CD is $500 - 100 = 400$ and IX is $10 - 1 = 9$

4 4071 •————

5 391254   All the other numbers are either too high or low.

6 5738 •———— If you subtract 4021 from 9759, you will be left with the missing number. $9759 - 4021 = 5738$

Page 23

Timed practice

1 a 1390   **b** 603   **c** 721   **d** 552

2 a 5005   **b** 1998   **c** 124   **d** 498

3 a 197   **b** DLXIX   **c** MXI

4 951

5 a 248   **b** 782   **c** 740

6 a 500   **b** 538   **c** 115

> **a** C = 100, XC = 90, VII = 7
> **b** D = 500, LX = 60, IX = 9
> **c** M = 1000, XI = 11

> Subtract the number of cars parked from the total number that the car park can hold.

> **a** Subtract 100 and add 8 back on.
> **b** Subtract 70 and then 2 more.
> **c** Add 600 and 100, then add 13 and 27

> **a** 1400 − 900 = 500
> The tens and ones remain unchanged.
> **b** 800 − 300 = 500 and 90 − 52 = 38
> **c** Count on 103 to 5000, then count on 12 more.

5 Column addition and subtraction

Page 25

Guided questions

1 £43.98

2 40 285

3 13 371

4 In the missing number squares : 29 466
final answer: 33 704

5 58 685

> You can't subtract 3 from 2, so you will need to borrow one from the tens of thousands column.

6 £4.66

> You need to subtract £15.34 from £20.00

Page 26

Have a go

1 4623

2 773

> 'Find the difference' means subtract the lower value number from the higher value number.

3 50 828

4 72 590

> First work out how many fiction books there are, then add together the numbers of fiction and non-fiction books.

5 12 933

> Subtract 567 from 13 500

Page 27

Timed practice

1 15 048

> 6000 + 348 + 8000 + 700

2 8864

> Subtract the smaller number from the larger number.

3 £11 740

> Subtract 13 499 from 25 239

4 31 708

> Subtract 2301 from 34 009

5 £878.38

> Add together £139.62 and £482, then subtract the total from £1500

6 a 1329

> Subtract the number of Bluebell Hill pupils from the number of St Kevin's pupils.

b 2666

> Add together the number of St Kevin's pupils and the number of Garden Lane School pupils.

6 Multiplication

Guided questions

1 A 700×300

2 a 26 **b** 3570 **c** 9150

> Move the digits to left when multiplying, once for ×10, twice for ×100, three times for ×1000

3 £24.95

4 0.63 and 630

> $0.09 \times 7 = 0.63$ and $90 \times 7 = 630$

5 470 750
13 450
484 200

6 300

> $6 \times 5 = 30$, so 60×5 is ten times larger.

Have a go

1 a 1200 **b** 600 **c** 63 **d** 46 000

> When multiplying by 10, 100 or 100, move the digits to the left.

2 a 18 **b** 1.8 **c** 180 **d** 1800

> Use the time table fact $3 \times 6 = 18$ to answer these questions.

3 £325

4 8680

> Divide 712 by 100 to get 7.12, then by 10 to get 0.712. Keith has multiplied his number by 1000

5 0.712

6 870

> Double the answer to the first calculation, because 145 doubled is 290

Timed practice

1 2040

> Use long multiplication.

2 $213 \times 1000 = 213\,000$

> Find half of $10 \times £0.36$

3 £1.80

4 100

> The digits have all moved 2 places left, therefore 45.60 has been multiplied by 100

5 174 177

6 £78.72

7 7.56

> Use long multiplication for this question, making sure that you position the decimal point correctly.

7 Division

Guided questions

> The answer is 6 r5, therefore 7 whole minibuses are needed. The seventh minibus would have some spare seats.

1 a 16 **b** 31 **c** 0.4

2 a 2.6 **b** 0.3 **c** 9.651

> Move digits to the right to divide by 10, 100 and 1000

3 $28\frac{4}{8}$ and 28 r4

> $228 \div 8 = 28$ r4 or 28 and four eighths

4

```
        4  4  r 6
  15 | 7  2  6
       6  0  0
       1  2  6
       1  2  0
             6
```

> You can share 726 into 48 equal shares of 15 with 6 left over.

5 34.6 r1 or 34.65

6 7 minibuses

Have a go

1. 4.72

2. 753 r7   or $753\frac{7}{9}$

3. 90 ————————— $63 \div 7 = 9$, so your answer must be 10 times larger than 9

4. **a** 100   **b** 10   **c** 1000

5. 69 ————————— There are no remainders in this calculation.

6. 3100 ————————— The population of Midtown is 31 000, and Littleburg has a population 10 times smaller than this.

Page 35

Timed practice

1. 946 r2

2. **a** 45.6   **b** 0.6325   **c** 98.564   **d** 5.001

3. £4 ————————— Divide £96 by 24

4. 333 ————————— You can divide this mentally using partitioning: $900 \div 3 = 300$, $90 \div 3 = 30$ and $9 \div 3 = 3$

5. 20 ————————— $163 \div 8 = 20$ r3

6. 4 ————————— All the other calculations result in an answer with a remainder.

7. There are <u>19</u> sweets in each bag with <u>2</u> left over.

Checkpoint 1

Page 36–37

1. 89 001

2. 4536, 45 036, 45 630, 450 036

3. **a** 9990   **b** 75 600   **c** 12 000

4. 1 °C

5. −6 °C   −3 °C   3 °C ————————— Negative numbers are to the left of zero on a number line. Positive numbers are to the right of zero on a number line.

6. 0.11, 0.15, 0.17 ————————— The sequence increases by 0.02 with each jump.

7. **a** 8   **b** 0.02   **c** 6.3

8. **a** Darren   **b** Peter ————————— 1.71 m is the highest jump and 1.62 m is the lowest jump.

9. **a** 1700   **b** 80 ————————— **a** M = 1000, DCC = 500 + 100 + 100 = 700   **b** L = 50, XXX = 30

10. 864

11. 25 856

12. **a** 860   **b** 56.3   **c** 5630

13. £28

14. 173 029

15. 80 ————————— 56 divided by 7 is 8
 560 divided by 7 is ten times larger.

16. 48 ————————— Short division gives the answer 48 r2, so 48 whole bags of 12 apples can be made with 2 apples left over.

8 Fractions

Page 39

Guided questions

1. **a** $\frac{3}{6} = \frac{1}{2}$ **b** $\frac{6}{10} = \frac{3}{5}$ **c** $\frac{2}{8} = \frac{1}{4}$

2 a 30   **b** 16

3 a $2\frac{3}{8}$ **b** $3\frac{3}{4}$

> There are enough quarters to make 3 whole ones, with 3 quarters left over.

4 $\frac{8}{10}$

> Multiply both the numerator and denominator by 2

5 a $\frac{2}{5}$ **b** $\frac{1}{10}$

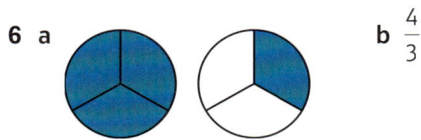

> Use common factors to simplify these fractions. 10 is a common factor of 10 and 100

6 a   **b** $\frac{4}{3}$

Page 40

Have a go

1 a 35   **b** 24

> **a** Both 7 and 20 can be multiplied by 5 to make $\frac{35}{100}$
>
> **b** Both 5 and 8 can be multiplied by 3 to make $\frac{15}{24}$

2 $\frac{5}{6}$

> All of the other fractions simplify to $\frac{1}{2}$

3 $\frac{1}{4}$

> The common factor of the numerator and the denominator is 12

4 a $1\frac{1}{2}$ **b** $\frac{6}{4}$ **c** $1\frac{3}{4}$ **d** $\frac{7}{4}$

5 a $\frac{19}{5}$ **b** $\frac{14}{6}$ **c** $\frac{9}{2}$

6 a $1\frac{2}{3}$ **b** $3\frac{1}{2}$ **c** $2\frac{1}{4}$

Page 41

Timed practice

1 $\frac{5}{20}$ C $\frac{8}{16}$ B $\frac{20}{60}$ D $\frac{12}{16}$ A

> Simplify the fractions to help you compare them to the diagrams.

2 a $\frac{3}{10}$ **b** $\frac{1}{2}$ **c** $\frac{2}{9}$

> Divide by the highest common factor.

3 $\frac{20}{24}$

> The other fractions can all be simplified to $\frac{4}{5}$

4 $\frac{2}{4}$ or $\frac{1}{2}$

5 a $\frac{7}{2}$ **b** $1\frac{1}{2}$ **c** $\frac{51}{10}$ **d** $\frac{7}{4}$ **e** $1\frac{4}{5}$

9 Percentages

Page 43

Guided questions

1 a Percentage: 30%, fraction: $\frac{30}{100}$

> Percent means out of 100, so you can write any percentage as a fraction out of 100

b Percentage: 26%, fraction: $\frac{26}{100}$

2 27

> Divide 54 by 2 to get 50%

3 90

> 10% of 300 is 30
> Three lots of this makes 30%.

4 a £15.00   **b** £28.80   **c** £12.00

> 10% of £15 is £1.50, so 20% is £3.00
> The price is reduced by £3, so it now costs £12

5 15% of 60

6 18

25% of 200 is 50 and 15% of 60 is 9

Page 44

Have a go

1 a 83% shaded and 17% unshaded

  b 11% shaded and 89% unshaded

$\frac{11}{100}$ is 11%. When you subtract this from 100, you are left with 89 unshaded squares.

2 22

3 45 g

10% of 300 g is 30 g and 5% is 15 g.

4 25% of 400

25% of 400 is 100, 10% of 600 is 60, 15% of 500 is 75 and 20% of 300 is 60

5 400 g

10% of 500 g is 50 g. Two slices must weigh 100 g, so there is 400 g left.

6 75%

There are $\frac{3}{4}$ unshaded. This can be converted to $\frac{75}{100}$ if you multiply both the denominator and numerator by 25

Page 45

Timed practice

1 12

10% of 40 is 4
Multiply this by 3 to find 30%.

2 18

Find 50% and 10% and add your answers together.

3 £17.50

4 10% of 66 = 6.6

10% of £25 is £2.50
30% = 3 × £2.50 = £7.50
Subtract this from the original price to find the sale price.

5 54

50% of 60 is 30, not 32 and 15% of 80 is 12, not 11

6 a 25%   **b** $\frac{25}{100}$ **c** 20%

  d $\frac{20}{100}$ **e** 75%   **f** $\frac{75}{100}$

30% of 120 is 36, 25% of 120 is 30
120 − 36 − 30 = 54

b $\frac{1}{4}$ is equivalent to $\frac{25}{100}$ **c** $\frac{1}{5}$ is equivalent to $\frac{20}{100}$ **e** $\frac{3}{4}$ is equivalent to $\frac{75}{100}$

10 Equivalence

Page 47

Guided questions

1 a $\frac{3}{20}$ **b** 5%   **c** 0.8

2 $\frac{1}{4}$

Justin has 25% left. This is equivalent to $\frac{25}{100}$ which simplifies to $\frac{1}{4}$

3 0.5 × 80

50% of 68 is 34
0.5 × 80 is the same as 50% of 80, which is 40.

4 40%

There are 8 slices left out of 20, which is $\frac{8}{20}$ as a fraction. You can convert this to $\frac{40}{100}$, which is 40%.

5 $\frac{1}{5}$ = 25%

Page 48

Have a go

$\frac{1}{5}$ is equivalent to 20% because it can be written as $\frac{20}{100}$

1 0.1 and $\frac{1}{10}$

0.1, $\frac{1}{10}$, $\frac{10}{100}$ and 10% are all equivalent.

2 0.2

$\frac{2}{10}$ can also be written as 0.2

3 25%; 0.75

4 0.90   0.89 $\dfrac{8}{10}$ 75%

0.25 can also be written as $\dfrac{25}{100}$ or 25%

75% can be written as $\dfrac{75}{100}$ or 0.75

5 12

10% have rabbits = 3 children

$\dfrac{1}{2}$ have cats = 15 children

$30 - 15 - 3 = 12$

Page 49
Timed practice

1 a 0.6   **b** 78%   **c** $\dfrac{21}{10}$ **d** 21%

$\dfrac{6}{10} = \dfrac{60}{100}$, so **a** is 0.6 or 0.60

2 $\dfrac{7}{10}$ and 70%

3 Fraction = $\dfrac{4}{10}$ or $\dfrac{2}{5}$ Decimal = 0.4   Percentage = 40%

8 out of 20 tiles are unshaded. $\dfrac{8}{20}$ can be converted to hundredths by multiplying by 5 to make $\dfrac{40}{100}$

This can be simplified to $\dfrac{4}{10}$

4 10% of 55 $\dfrac{2}{10}$ of 30 0.6×50

5 25%

$\dfrac{3}{5} = \dfrac{6}{10} = \dfrac{60}{100} = 60\%$

60% + 15% = 75%

25% is left for onions.

6 20%

There are 25 pupils altogether

$\dfrac{5}{25}$ travel by car. $\dfrac{5}{25} = \dfrac{20}{100} = 20\%$

11 Ratio and proportion

Page 51
Guided questions

1 c 3:1

Simplify 12:4 by dividing both sides of the ratio by 4

2 c 16:32

There are 3 parts in total. $48 \div 3 = 16$, so 1 part is worth 16 and 2 parts are worth 32

3 a 2:3   **b** 12

To convert the ratio 2:3 to ?:18, you must multiply both numbers by 6, which gives 12 white tiles for every 18 blue tiles.

Page 52
Have a go

1 2:3

Divide 6:9 by 3, the highest common factor of this pair of numbers.

2 1:4

The question asks for the number of fluorescent pens first. Use the HCF 4 to simplify the ratio.

3 36

The time has been multiplied by 12, so multiply the number of cars by 12 as well.

4 a 4:20   **b** 6:18   **c** 16:8

a There are 6 parts, so each one is worth 4
b There are 4 parts, so each one is worth 6
c There are 12 parts, so each one is worth 2

5 300 g

Page 53
Timed practice

Write the number of white gerbils first. The highest common factor used for simplifying is 2

1 8:7

There are 11 stripy fish and 16 spotty ones. This ratio can't be simplified because the HCF of 11 and 16 is 1

2 16:11

3 Sarah gets 15 apples; Carla gets 10 apples

There are 5 shares in the ratio 3:2, so each share is worth 5
Sarah gets $2 \times 5 = 10$, and Carla gets $3 \times 5 = 15$

4 9

The number of blue cars has been multiplied by 3, so do the same to the number of red cars.

5 300 g

> The amount of orange flavour has been multiplied by 3, so do the same to the amount of cocoa.

6 18

> The number of wins has been multiplied by 6, so do the same to the losses.

12 Scale factors

Page 55
Guided questions

1 5

> The sides of the shape have increased from 2 cm to 10 cm. They have been multiplied by 5

2

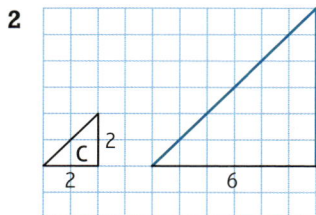

> The sides were 2 squares. A scale factor of 3 means you multiply all measurements by 3

3 $a = 8$ cm $b = 24$ cm $c = 32$ cm

> A scale factor of 4 means you multiply all the sides by 4

4

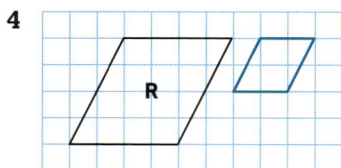

> A scale factor of 0.5 means that the enlarged shape will be half the original size.

5 $A = 4$ cm $B = 1$ cm

> Both the measurements must be divided by 5, as the scale factor was 5

Page 56
Have a go

1 4

> 3 cm × 4 = 12 cm, so a scale factor of 4 has been used.

2 Shape **Y**

> The shape **Y** has sides 3 times longer than shape **Z**.

3 $a = 10$ $b = 50$ $c = 40$

> $a = 2 \times 5 = 10$; $b = 10 \times 5 = 50$; $c = 8 \times 5 = 40$

4 75 cm

> Multiply the length of the box by 5

Page 57
Timed practice

1 2

> Both measurements have been increased by a scale factor of 2

2 $a = 15$ $b = 6$ $c = 9$

> Each number has been multiplied by 1.5
> You can do this mentally by halving the number and adding half on to the original number.

3 B (13, 15) C (13, 3) D (5, 3)

> The new rectangle will be 8 wide by 12 long. Read the x-axis first, then the y-axis.

4 The mural will be <u>125 cm</u> tall and <u>105 cm</u> wide.

Checkpoint 2

Page 58–59

1 $\dfrac{11}{4}$

> In two whole ones, there are 8 quarters. 8 + 3 = 11 quarters in total.

2 $3\dfrac{2}{3}$

> 3 thirds are needed to make a whole. From 11 thirds, you can make 3 whole ones with 2 thirds left over.

3 $\dfrac{6}{18}$ and $\dfrac{1}{3}$

> Dividing $\dfrac{6}{18}$ by 6 gives $\dfrac{1}{3}$

4 a $\frac{1}{2}$ **b** $\frac{1}{6}$ **c** $\frac{1}{5}$ ●————— Divide by common factors to simplify

5 a 0.95 **b** 33% **c** $\frac{56}{100}$ ●————— Percentages show how many parts out of 100 you have. This can be written as a fraction out of 100 or as hundredths using place value.

6 18.5

7 78 ●————— 50% of 130 is 65
10% of 130 is 13, so 60% is 78

8 £10.20 ●————— 10% of £12 is £1.20 and 5% is £0.60, meaning that the scarf has been reduced by £1.80

9 a 7.2 **b** 25% **c** $\frac{3}{10}$ ●————— **a** $\frac{72}{100} = 0.72\%$ **b** $\frac{1}{5} = \frac{20}{100}$ **c** $0.03 = 3\%$

10 a >
b =
c <
●————— **a** 0.01 is equivalent to 1% which is less than 10%.
b Both amounts are worth a half.
c 95% is equivalent to 0.95, which is less than 0.99

11 3:1

12 39 ●————— A ratio of 1:3 means there are 4 parts in total. 52 divided by 4 is 13 You can use this to work out Maimuna's share.

13 3 ●————— The length and width of the rectangle have both been multiplied by 3

14 30 cm ●————— 5 cm multiplied by 6 is 30 cm.

13 Converting units

Page 61

Have a go

1 2500 ml ●————— To convert litres to millilitres, multiply by 1000

2 20 ●————— 2 m = 200 cm. 10 cm fits into 200 cm 20 times.

3 1250 g and 1.25 kg ●————— $5 \times 250 \, g = 1250 \, g = 1.25 \, kg$

4 16 400 m ●————— Convert kilometres to metres by multiplying by 1000

5 10 kg ●————— $200 \, g \times 50 = 10 \, 000 \, g = 10 \, kg$

6 300 hours ●————— There are 12 months in a year. $12 \times 25 = 300$

7 25.6 km ●————— Convert miles into kilometres by multiplying by 1.6
$16 \times 1.5 = 24$, so 25.6 is the most sensible answer

8 49 minutes ●————— 1 hour 38 minutes is equal to 98 minutes. $98 \div 2 = 49$

Page 62

Have a go

1 32 cm ●————— Convert millimetres to centimetres by dividing by 10

2 6 weeks ●————— There are 7 days in a week. $43 \div 2 = 6 \, r1$, so Dillon goes to the gym every day for 6 whole weeks.

3 a 1.5 l **b** 1500 ml ●—————
4 8200 m
●————— 3 litres = 3000 ml. Half of this is 1.5 l or 1500 ml.

5 250 g, 0.25 kg ●————— $10 \times 25 \, g = 250 \, g$. This can be converted to kilograms by dividing by 1000

6 4.2 m ●————— $4200 \div 1000 = 4.2$

7 150 g ●————— $25 \, g \approx 1 \, oz$. $25 \times 6 = 150$

Have a go

1 **a** 2000 mm   **b** 150 000 cm   **c** 20 m

2 4 years

3 **a** 0.9 l   **b** 900 ml

4 1050 g

5 30 cm, 0.3 m

6 50 cm

7 804 km

> There are 12 months in 1 year. $12 \times 4 = 48$

> 3×300 ml $= 900$ ml which is equal to 0.9 l

> There are 21 days in 3 weeks.
> $10 \times 50 = 500$ and $20 \times 50 = 1000$
> $1000 + 50 = 1050$

> 300 mm $= 30$ cm $= 0.3$ m

> 1 inch ≈ 2.5 cm
> 10×2.5 cm $= 25$ cm
> 20×2.5 cm $= 50$ cm

> Approximately convert miles to kilometres by multiplying by 1.5
> $500 \times 1.5 = 750$, so 804 km is the closest answer.

14 Perimeter

Guided questions

1 60 cm

2 34 cm

3 58 cm

4 74 cm

5 30 cm

> To find the perimeter add the side lengths together or multiply one side length by 4

> $5 + 8 + 3 + 5 + 3 + 8 + 5 + 8 + 5 + 8 = 58$

> $5 + 9 + 4 + 9 + 7 + 12 + 16 + 12 = 74$

> There are four equal sides in a square. 1.2 m $= 120$ cm.
> 120 cm $\div 4 = 30$ cm.

Have a go

1 **A** 16 cm   **B** 18 cm   **C** 8 cm

2 200 m

3 74 cm

4 B

5 whole lengths: 3; left over: 8 m

6 44 cm

> Four equal sides of 50 m makes 200 m in total.

> Two sides of 22 cm makes 44 cm. Two sides of 15 makes 30 cm.
> $44 + 30 = 74$ cm

> **B** has a perimeter of 32 units.

> The perimeter of the allotment is 22 m, so Sarah must buy 3 lengths of fencing. There will be 8 m spare.

> The vertical sides add up to 24 cm, the horizontal sides add up to 20 cm.

Timed practice

1 **A** 14 cm   **B** 22 cm   **C** 28 cm

2 144 m

3 32 cm

4 D

5 3.6 m

6 3 m

> The perimeter of one lap is 48 m. $3 \times 48 = 144$ m

> 3 sides of 4 cm $= 12$ cm, 2 sides of 5 cm $= 10$ cm, 2 sides of 3 cm $= 6$ cm. The missing side is 4 cm. $12 + 10 + 6 + 4 = 32$ cm.

> The other 3 shapes all have a perimeter of 16 units.

> The perimeter is 360 cm. 3.6 m is equal to 360 cm.

> There are 2 sides with length 7 m. Subtract 14 from 20 to get 6. This is the length of 2 sides, so the answer is 3 m each.

15 Area

Guided questions

1 84 cm²

> $12 \times 7 = 84$

2 35 m² ●——————————————————● Area = length × width. 7 m × 5 m = 35 m²

3 The 4 × 6 rectangle and the 2 × 12 rectangle. ●————● Both these shapes have areas of 24
2 × 12 = 24 and 4 × 6 = 24

4 a 96 cm²　　**b** 36 cm　　**c** 9 cm ●————————● 8 × 12 = 96
10 + 10 + 8 + 8 = 36

5 a 4500 m²　　**b** 1125 ●
The pitch is 90 m × 50 m = 4500 m² and each square is 4 m².
4500 m² ÷ 4 m² = 1125, so Henry needs 1125 squares of artificial turf.

6 36 cm² ●

Page 70

Have a go

1 A 18 cm²　　**B** 9 cm²　　**C** 12 cm²

Both 6.3 and 5.8 round to 6
6 × 6 = 36

2 117 m² ●————————————————● 9 m × 13 m = 117 m²

3 10.5 m² ●————————————————● 3.5 × 3 = 10.5

4 A ●————————————————● A has an area of 12 squares, **B** is 9 squares and **C** is 6 squares.

5 8 m ●————————————————● 12 × 8 = 96, so 8 m is the missing measurement.

6 108 m² ●————————————————● Round the measurements to 12 m and 9 m

Page 71

Timed practice

1 a 2 mm　　**b** 5 m　　**c** 96 cm² ●————● Area = width × length. Write area using squared units.

2 a 52 cm²　　**b** 42 cm²　　**c** 21 cm²

b and **d** both have an area of 16
a, **b** and **c** all have a perimeter of 20

3 a **b** and **d**　　**b** **a**, **b** and **c** ●

4 2 m ●————————————————● Divide 3 by 1.5 to find the length of the mats.

5 1200 m² ●————————————————● Round 56.8 to 60 and 20.2 to 20

6 6 cm × 0.10 m and 3 cm × 20 cm ●————● 6 cm × 0.10 m = 60 cm² because 0.10 m is the same as 10 cm.
3 cm × 20 cm = 60 cm².

16 Reflections and Translations

Page 73

Guided questions

1

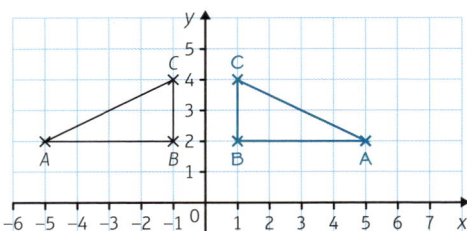

Point *C* will be plotted at (1, 4) as the *y*-axis is the mirror line.

2

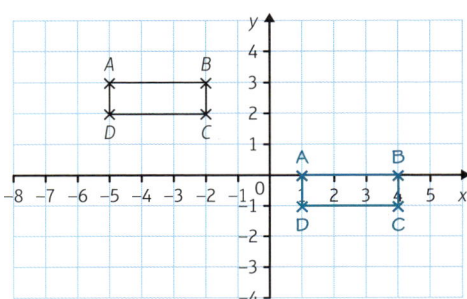

All the points of the rectangle have moved right by 6 squares.

3 D (−2, −7)

To read coordinates, first check the *x*-axis (horizontal), then the *y*-axis (vertical).

4 A True   **B** False   **C** True

B has been reflected in the *y*-axis

Page 74
Have a go

1

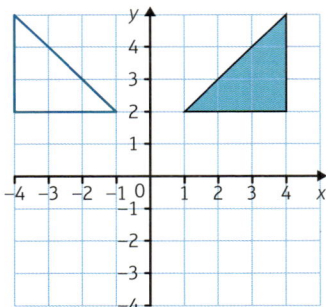

Use the *y*-axis as the mirror line.

2 a False   **b** True   **c** False

a Reflected shapes remain congruent.
b Translated shapes also remain congruent.
c The *x*-axis is horizontal.

3

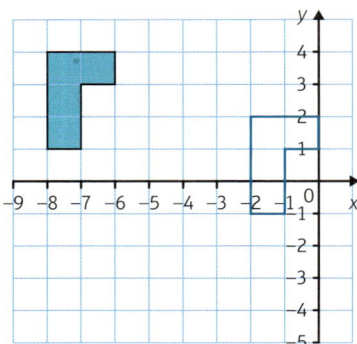

The shape has been moved 6 squares to the right and 2 squares down.

4 a reflected   **b** reflection in the *x*-axis

The shape has been flipped horizontally, so the *x*-axis is the mirror line.

5 B and **C**

The other shapes have been translated or rotated.

6 R4, D4

The shape has been translated 4 squares right and then 4 squares down.

Page 75
Timed practice

1

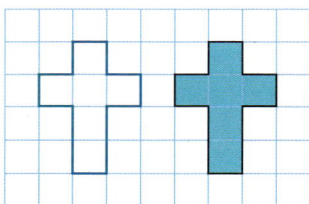

The shape has been translated 4 squares to the left.

2 A (−6, 1) B (3, 6) C (2, −4) D (−3,−3)

To read coordinates, first check the *x*-axis, then the *y*-axis.

3 A (5, 1) B (4, 2) C (2, 2) D (1, 1)

Reflection means the shape is flipped, so points A and B will now be on the right hand side, instead of the left.

4 A = translation; **B** = reflection; **C** = translation

Reflections are shapes which have been flipped over, and translations are when the shape is simply moved.

5 The two triangles

All the other shapes have changed size and shape.

6 A (−6, −4) B (−4, −5) C (−2, −4) D (−4, −1)

All the coordinate points are now in the bottom right portion of the grid where the coordinates are all negative.

Checkpoint 3

Page 76–77

1 73 000 ml

1 litre is equal to 1000 ml, so 73 l = 73 000 ml.

2 20 m ●────────── To convert centimetres into metres, divide by 100

3 10 inches ●────── To convert centimetres to inches, divide by 2.5
1 inch ≈ 2.5 cm

4 45 km ●────────── To roughly convert miles to kilometres, multiply by 1.5

5 56 days ●───────── There are 7 days in one week. $7 \times 8 = 56$

6 1.25 hours ●─────── 1 hour = 60 minutes, so 74 minutes is 1 hour and 14 minutes.

7 60 m ●──────────── A square has four equal sides. $4 \times 15 = 60$

8 28 cm ●─────────── To find the perimeter, add together the side lengths. The longer
unlabelled side = 7 cm + 3 cm. The short unlabelled side = 2 cm + 2 cm.

9 5 ●────────────── The perimeter of the field is $4 \times 24 = 96$ m. Sam will need to buy 5 lengths
of 20 m, but will have 4 m left over.

10 6.4 m^2 ●──────── Area = length × width. 80 cm = 0.8 m. $8 \text{ m} \times 0.8 \text{ m} = 6.4 \text{ m}^2$

11 a C   **b** D ●──── Shape **C** has an area of 40 units² and Shape **D** has an area of 12 units².

12 a False   **b** True   **c** False

13 R2, D2 ●────────── The shape has moved right 2 squares and down 2 squares.

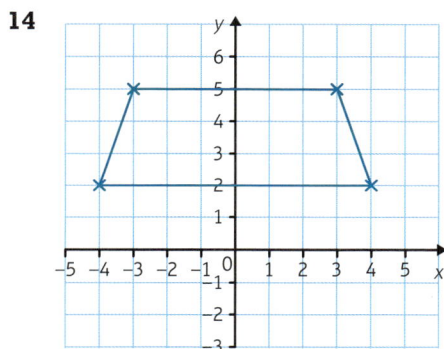

14

Remember to plot coordinates using the *x*-axis first, then
the *y*-axis.

Progress test

Page 78–83

8948 only has 4 digits so is the lowest value, all the others have 5 or 6
Check the value of each digit, working from right to left.

1 894 798   89 897   89 798   8948 ●

2 a 8000   **b** 587 120   **c** 10 000 ●

a Round down to 8000 as there are 2 hundreds.
b Round up to 587 120 as there are 5 ones.
c Round up to 10 000 as there are 9 thousands.

3 42 °C ●──────────── Count 12 °C back to zero and add 30 °C.

4 −15   −8   −5   12 ●── Negative numbers with a larger digit have a lower value as they are
further from zero.

5 d 5.689 to the nearest tenth = 5.6 ●

5.689 rounds to 5.7 because there are 8 hundredths.

6 a James   **b** Bert ●──── James' and Bert's times are the slowest and third slowest.

7 a LVI   **b** CX ●

50 is L, VI is 6
M = c = 100 and X = 10

8 590 ●

Use the inverse operation of addition: mentally subtract 405 from 995
Check your answer by adding 590 + 405 = 995

9 £14 452 — Using column addition: $5300 + 9152 = 14\,452$

10 3233 — Using column subtraction: $15\,533 - 12\,300 = 3233$

11 a 36 500   **b** 156.3   **c** 15 630 — Multiplying by 10 means all digits move one place to the left.

12 £43.50

13 9

14 3276

15 5 coaches — There are 150 passengers including the adults. Long division gives the answer: $150 \div 35 = 4$ r10. 5 coaches would be required.

16 $5\frac{1}{5}$ — 5 fifths are needed to make a whole one. From 26 fifths you can make 5 whole ones with 1 fifth left over.

17 $\frac{6}{9}$ — $\frac{6}{9}$ can be simplified to $\frac{2}{3}$ using the highest common factor 3

18 a $\frac{1}{4}$ **b** $\frac{1}{20}$ **c** $\frac{3}{5}$

19 a $\frac{99}{100}$ **b** 10%   **c** 45%

20 75% — $\frac{5}{20} = \frac{1}{4} = 25\%$, so 75% of the fish are not stripy.

21 20% — $\frac{3}{5} = \frac{6}{10} = \frac{60}{100} = 60\%$. $60\% + 20\% = 80\%$, therefore the remaining 20% of the marbles are yellow.

22 1.5   15% $\frac{1}{5}$ 0.22

23 3:2 — 9 tabby kittens to 6 black kittens can be simplified from 9:6 to 3:2 using the highest common factor 3

24 a 8:24 — There are 4 parts in total. Each part is worth 8 because $32 \div 4 = 8$. One part is 8 and 3 parts are 24

b 12:20 — There are 8 parts in total, so each part is worth 4. 3 parts are 12 and 5 parts are 20

25 3

26 length = 30 cm; width = 17.5 cm — To find the original width: $84 \div 12 = 7$. $12 \times 2.5 = 30$ and $7 \times 2.5 = 17.5$

27 25 500 ml — The are 1000 ml in 1 l. Convert 25.5 l to millilitres by multiplying by 1000

28 5500 m — Convert kilometres to metres by multiplying by 1000

29 7 ounces — There are roughly 25 g in 1 ounce. $175 \div 25 = 7$

30 1 hour 45 minutes — 3×35 minutes $= 105$ minutes, which is one hour and 45 minutes.

31 28 cm — The missing lengths can be worked out using the measurements on the opposite side of the shape.

32 3.36 m — Add together 2×123 and 2×45. Convert centimetres to metres by dividing by 100

33 91 m²

34 a R2   **b** R1, U3   **c** R1, D2 — Record movements right as 'R', movements left as 'L', up as 'U' and down as 'D'.

35 A (−4, −3) B (−4, 2)
C (4, 1) D (4, −2)

> Read along the x-axis first, then up or down the y-axis.

36

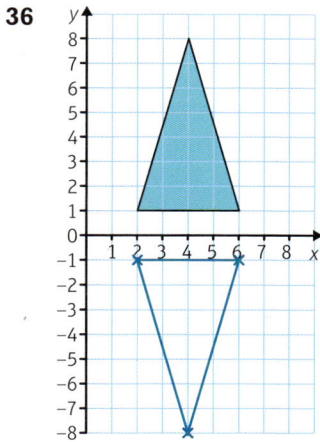

> The x-axis runs horizontally.

Published by Pearson Education Limited, 80 Strand, London, WC2R 0RL.

www.pearsonschools.co.uk

Text © Pearson Education Limited 2018
Edited, typeset and produced by Elektra Media Ltd
Original illustrations © Pearson Education Limited
Illustrated by Elektra Media Ltd
Cover design by Lukas Bischoff

The right of Rebecca Corden to be identified as author of this work has been asserted by her in accordance with the Copyright, Designs and Patents Act 1988.

First published 2018

21 20 19 18
10 9 8 7 6 5 4 3 2 1

British Library Cataloguing in Publication Data
A catalogue record for this book is available from the British Library

ISBN: 978 1 292 24648 2

Printed in Slovakia by Neografia

Acknowledgements
We would like to thank Nik Prowse and Amanda Booth for their invaluable help in the development and trialling of this publication.

Note from the publisher
Pearson has robust editorial processes, including answer and fact checks, to ensure the accuracy of the content in this publication, and every effort is made to ensure this publication is free of errors. We are, however, only human, and occasionally errors do occur. Pearson is not liable for any misunderstandings that arise as a result of errors in this publication, but it is our priority to ensure that the content is accurate. If you spot an error, please do contact us at resourcescorrections@pearson.com so we can make sure it is corrected.

Progress chart

Use this chart to keep track of your 11+ journey. Fill in your marks as you complete each *Timed practice* section and check off any extra practice you do.

	Timed practice	Digital questions	Ten-minute test
Diagnostic test	☐ / 52		
1 Ordering and rounding numbers	☐ / 13	☑	☑
2 Negative numbers	☐ / 15	☑	☑
3 Decimal numbers	☐ / 12	☑	☑
4 Mental addition and subtraction	☐ / 18	☑	☑
5 Column addition and subtraction	☐ / 7	☑	☑
6 Multiplication	☐ / 7	☑	☑
7 Division	☐ / 10	☑	☑
Checkpoint 1	☐ / 28	☑	
8 Fractions	☐ / 14	☑	☑
9 Percentages	☐ / 11	☑	☑
10 Equivalence	☐ / 12	☑	☑
11 Ratio and proportion	☐ / 7	☑	☑
12 Scale factors	☐ / 9	☑	☑
Checkpoint 2	☐ / 22	☑	
13 Converting units	☐ / 11	☑	☑
14 Perimeter	☐ / 8	☑	☑
15 Area	☐ / 11	☑	☑
16 Reflections and translations	☐ / 13	☑	☑
Checkpoint 3	☐ / 20	☑	
Progress test	☐ / 53	☑	